THE PREGNANT COUPLE'S GUIDE TO SEX, ROMANCE, AND INTIMACY

THE PREGNANT COUPLE'S GUIDE TO SEX, ROMANCE, AND INTIMACY

Sandra Margot

with Deborah Herman and Tonianne Robino

CITADEL PRESS
Kensington Publishing Corp.
www.kensingtonbooks.com

CITADEL PRESS BOOKS are published by

Kensington Publishing Corp.
850 Third Avenue
New York, NY 10022

All Kensington titles, imprints, and distributed lines are available at special quantity discounts for bulk purchases for sales promotions, premiums, fund-raising, educational, or institutional use. Special book excerpts or customized printings can also be created to fit specific needs. For details, write or phone the office of the Kensington special sales manager: Kensington Publishing Corp., 850 Third Avenue, New York, NY 10022, attn: Special Sales Department, phone 1-800-221-2647.

CITADEL PRESS is Reg. U.S. Pat. & TM Off.
The Citadel Logo is a trademark of Kensington Publishing Corp.

First printing: September 2002

10 9 8 7 6 5 4 3 2 1

Designed by Leonard Telesca

Printed in the United States of America

Library of Congress Control Number: 2001099134

ISBN 0-8065-2323-9

This book is dedicated to the most beautiful woman in the world: my mother, Dianna. For it is only through her amazing inner strength, endless courage, and unconditional love and acceptance that I am the person I am today. I love you, Mom.

Contents

Acknowledgments

This book would not have been possible without the support of the following people, and I'd like them to know just how integral they were to this project by acknowledging them here. . . . First of all, thanks to Deborah Herman and Tonianne Robino, my dedicated coauthors. Without the two of you, this book would never have happened. You gave it that certain "je ne sais quoi"—THANK YOU! I would also like to give a big "Thanks!" to my agent, Sherri Spillane, who never stopped believing in me no matter how crazy I made her over the past few years! To my two beautiful daughters, Sabree Lane and Ever Skye, you were Mommy's "inspiration" for this book and I love you both more than I could ever express in black and white. To Hedda Muskat, a very close and dear friend who believed in me and pushed me in the direction of this book . . . you saw something in me from day one, even when I didn't see it in myself, and for that I am thankful. To my grandma, Melba "Moo Moo" Gunter; my best friend, Pietta Mia Allenstein (Menosse); and Felix "Uncle Phil" Voza . . . three people whom I love and adore and who have been my "anchors" throughout my life. I love the three of you as if you were blood relatives and you will always hold a special place in my heart. And last but certainly not least . . . to my loving husband, Ron Escott. Your love and devotion are unlike any I've ever known, and we shall be together throughout eternity. I love you.

Sandra Margot

Chapter One

Pregnancy Panic and the Joys of Pregnant Sex

There you are—in your bathroom urinating on a stick that will determine your fate. You turn away as you count the requisite minutes. In a few moments the die will be cast. You open your eyes. The results say you are pregnant. "Yes!!" you exclaim.

You dial your husband. No, this is too important to waste on a phone call, so you hang up. You rush to the grocery store to prepare his favorite dinner. Instead of a bottle of wine, you buy a bottle of sparkling cider. How to tell him? You stop in the baby section of the store and buy a rattle. You put it in a gift bag with a note telling your husband how much you love him and how your dreams are coming true.

Dinner is lovely and your husband comments about the Cheshire cat grin on your face. You are surprised at your restraint. You bring out the cider and pour it into champagne flutes.

"What is the occasion?" your husband asks.

"Oh nothing special," you reply, not very convincingly.

You give him your gift and watch expectantly as he unwraps the clue to his future. At first it doesn't register. Then his mouth drops open and he begins to cry. He puts his arms around you and draws your mouth to his. You have never known such happiness or desire.

You kiss hungrily and walk blindly toward the bedroom. You fall back onto the bed and just as the clothes come off you both stop, pause, and exclaim, "We're going to have a baby?"

*   *   *

Very few life events will have the impact that becoming pregnant will have on you and your mate. Men and women react differently to the process, but the emotions are similar. The primary emotion, other than joy, is most certainly fear. The miracle of pregnancy is also the mystery of life. You will be in awe of the meaning of it, but when the reality sets in it is perfectly natural to be terrified. You may be surrounded with "myth-information." There are more superstitions and old wives' tales about pregnancy and childbirth than you can imagine. You will also be facing many emotions and issues that you may not even know you have.

Pregnancy can be a glorious time of bonding and intimacy for a couple; but if a couple is not careful, it can also be a miserable time that can make a troubled relationship even worse. The goal of this book is to help you and your mate make the most of this miraculous time you share. These nine months on the road to parenthood can be magical if you have the right attitude, the right information, and some really good sex.

This book is a guide for couples, but women will undoubtedly be more interested in certain subjects than the men in their lives will be. So, men, feel free to skip the parts that don't seem to apply. Just make sure you don't skip the parts that can teach you to be a more open and skilled lover. Your spouse may not be able to tell you directly that your love-making needs improvement. Believe me, the need for improvement is not a reflection on your manhood. Most men are not fluent in the language of pleasing their mate, especially because women often know less about their bodies than men do.

I have counseled many clients in my work as a sexologist, so I know there are many techniques you can master that will have your woman . . . well you get the picture. Don't worry, I will give her some great tips, too. I will fill you both in on some secrets that you can use even after the baby is grown and out of the house. As you will learn, sex during pregnancy has many long-term rewards for your relationship. However, good love-making is forever.

When a couple discovers they are pregnant their emotions will shift back and forth from elation to panic to elation. It is best to accept the changes as they come and not project so much into the future. This is, of course, not an easy task. Getting married is a big step, but having a baby means that you must put away the things of childhood. In theory, you must now grow up and become responsible.

"Responsible" is such a dirty word. It conjures images of station wagons, too many bills, a boring existence, and, for many, the end of a quality sex life. As you work through having a baby together, one of the greatest rites of passage into adulthood, you can develop a relationship beyond your expectations. Now is the time to do this. Now is the time to assess your needs and the needs of your mate and to determine how this mixture of needs can be met.

When you are in the process of becoming parents, try not to forget that your relationship came first. You were attracted to each other by appearance, personality, or, as some scientists believe, each other's scent. Seriously. Many Eastern mystics also believe that men and women can smell each other on a very subtle level, which often creates their animal attraction. This is why yogis suggest that you include kissing and caressing at the hairline in your foreplay. They believe this is a good place to experience the subtle odors that heighten your connection and arousal.

Never forget that you were lovers before you were partners on this parental path. A marriage or any relationship requires balance, but, surprisingly enough, people sometimes dismiss the importance of sex in the scheme of a flourishing relationship. We are all so mixed up about it. We may even feel that sex is the domain of the carefree. We many think of pregnancy and the new responsibilities of parenthood as a time when we must put aside our sexual needs. Both men and women change their perspectives of each other when they view the other as "parent." I can't stress enough how unbalanced your relationship will become if you do not put enough energy into maintaining a thriving sex life.

As promised, this book is about sex and we will spend a lot of time talking about it. But it is also about intimacy. The two go hand in hand. You may not need or even desire intimacy in a relationship that is not fully committed. Marriage doesn't guarantee that either spouse feels totally committed even if they are monogamous in behavior. But if you are forming a family and want to stay together to raise your child, you must look at what will bring you closer together. The fantasy of raising a baby together is glorious. The reality, while wonderful and fulfilling, is a lot of work. Sometimes the only reward is knowing that you are loved and cared for by each other. Your sex life will support this and may be your ticket to sanity.

So use this time to "grow" together. Although sex is more challenging with a woman's ever-changing shape, the experience of loving each other through sex during this time will be worth the efforts you need to make. There are many reasons why sex is an important link between a man and a woman in general, and a pregnant couple specifically. One of them is how much more complicated human beings are than other mammals. This is not always to our advantage and I often wonder which creatures are the more enlightened. As far as we know, most species mate according to instincts. Human beings do, too, but we also throw a lot of emotion, hang-ups, and analysis into the mix.

Have you ever known an animal, other than human beings, to be so concerned with the size of the "royal member"? Have you ever heard of another creature worried about whether or not they are able to please their mate? It is "do it and do it again" for most creatures until the deed is accomplished.

We bring so many issues into the bedroom that it is amazing that any of us has sex with the same person twice. When you fall in love and make a commitment you can be lulled into the false sense of security that love and orgasm can conquer all. It can conquer most things if it is handled in a way that is satisfying and fulfilling for both partners. Sex together is not going to be like the first time very time. In my opinion it gets better with time with the same person because the more you know about one another and the more you trust each other the more you are willing to explore what makes each of you happiest. But we can't always help comparing that first blush of lust and infatuation with the realities of having a life together.

When we get to know each other and add the element of friendship, other issues kick in. Sex, after all, begins in the mind, so if your mind is straightened out and if you have a good idea about what goes on in the sexual part of your marriage, you stand a better chance of keeping your relationship healthy and your marriage thriving. Never forget that your marriage is a business as well as the joining of two bodies with passion and lover's insanity. When you become pregnant together you are adding a new "department" to the "business." You want to make sure that your other "departments" are still working smoothly.

Let me put it more simply. "If you don't use it you are going to lose it." When you are married and you get pregnant and have a baby together your roles will change. You might even find that you become closer friends. Friendship is a wonderful and sustaining thing, but it does not necessarily get the juices flowing. A bottle of wine (before you get pregnant) can help, but without the sexual spark you won't ever be able to kindle the flame. Human beings need sex. If you begin to see your lover as merely a friend or a co-parent, you may find yourself hitting the chocolate, fantasizing, or acting out in all sorts of ways.

You are going to start looking for a substitute. Many people like the Internet, which, as titillating as it can be, is not a good way to strengthen a relationship. When you fantasize online, you are having fun but you are using up energy that you could share with your spouse. There is only so much sexual energy to go around. Your goal is to build up the excitement between each other; otherwise you are going to be perpetually frustrated. Sex begins in the mind, so if your mind is somewhere else—let's say in a chatroom—you are chipping away at your connection.

Some men think a pregnant wife is a perfect excuse for "getting something on the side." Internet play, phone sex, or even a trip to the strip club does not help your connection with your loved one. Recreational fantasy is fun, but during this time you do not want to be reinforcing your desire for someone else. You might decide to act on it, and that would be a very dumb move. You would be destroying a tenuous bond that will set the tone for your relationship as parents. You don't want to bring a baby into that. If you and your wife do not trust each other, you are going to face many difficulties.

So don't do anything stupid. Learn to keep sex at home and learn how to please each other. Women especially should not have their natural insecurities reinforced during this delicate time. Imagine a pumpkin growing inside of you and see how much you would appreciate your wife eyeing another guy. Your role as a husband is to make your wife feel like The Madonna and Madonna all rolled into one.

But if you do not put a priority on sex during this time you are both going to find ways to distract yourself or to meet your needs head-on. Both men and women can be led by their drives to make half-baked decisions. I will show you how to keep things *hot* even if you are feeling *not*. With the right attitude you can keep the insecurities, fears, and misconceptions out of your bed.

You can be friends, partners, co-parents, and lovers all at the same time.

Making Your Bed

Back to our story:

You are holding on to each other for dear life. It is starting to sink in that you are going to become parents. You want to make love but you can't stop thinking about your own parents. You always thought of them as being so old. Your husband plays with your breasts. Sex always has a way of calming his nerves, but you find yourself unresponsive.

He flicks his tongue on your nipples and even though you feel that rush of excitement in your loins, you feel paralyzed. You didn't like your childhood. Your parents fought a lot and you thought they were too strict. You always thought you would do things differently but now you are not sure. What if your husband becomes like your father was? You remember him working late and always complaining how difficult it was to support the family.

Well if you had read this book ahead of time you would already know that allowing these issues into your bed is like emotionally painting yourself into a corner. You are not going to be able to resolve all your fears in one night. You will want to confront them preferably when you have clothes on and your husband is not sucking on your breasts.

You dismiss your thoughts and give in to the pleasure you are feeling from your husband's gentle touch and you respond with soft murmurs of delight. You reach over to kiss him and you see a strange look in his eyes. He has stopped caressing you and seems far away. You have seen this look before. In fact you saw it just about a half hour ago after the news settled in.

*   *   *

As the husband, all sorts of things are running through your mind. You may not yet be thinking about such practical issues as how are you going to pay for things. You may be worried about how to make love to your wife now that she is carrying a new life inside her. You are worried that if you are too rough you will hurt the baby. You have known couples who have lost their babies in the early stages of pregnancy and you are worried that your penis could somehow knock the baby out of the uterus.

You gently caress her tummy and see that she does not understand your hesitation. You rest your head there, as if you are listening for a sign of life. You want her more than ever, but hold back. You can't stop worrying. That is your baby in there.

Don't be afraid to celebrate your good news with sex. In the following chapters, you will read about many myths associated with sex during pregnancy. In most situations, unless a woman has been found to be a high risk (which is something your obstetrician will tell you or that you will know before conception) your sex life can continue pretty much as it did before pregnancy. As the pregnancy progresses you may need to make adjustments for obvious reasons, but you can enjoy a full and satisfying sex life all through the pregnancy and beyond. Rest assured that you will not hurt the baby by making love. Nothing will break and the baby is not going to know that his parents are fooling around. The baby can't see her daddy's penis and, in fact, probably likes the rocking motion of intercourse.

It is natural to be concerned about miscarriage in the first months of pregnancy. Miscarriages will happen in a certain number of pregnancies for many reasons that have nothing to do with sexual intercourse. Sometimes a miscarriage is Nature's way of compensating for something that is simply not right. There may be something innately wrong with the pregnancy that has nothing to do with the mother. Sex will not cause miscarriage, and it should not be avoided during this period of important bonding for you and your spouse.

If you are still afraid to take a chance, wait to meet with an obstetrician before you engage in penetration. Fear is definitely an anti-aphrodisiac, so it is best to wait until you can be comfortable and mentally engaged. No one expects either of you to know what is going to happen during your pregnancy. This is new territory and it is perfectly normal to have a million questions. Your obstetrician is there to guide you emotionally as well as medically. It is very beneficial for a father-to-be to attend the first appointment with his wife and as many appointments as possible until delivery and even during follow-up. Both husband and wife need to know what is going on inside the woman's body. This will not only help the process, but also be a reassurance that sex is okay.

The different stages of pregnancy have their own physical and emotional issues. One week the mother-to-be is "not interested" and the next week her tired husband has to lock himself in the bathroom to get any rest.

Having a baby together is a wondrous journey. As lovers it is a time for you to explore. This time before the baby is born is in fact the last time for a while when you will be truly alone. When you have children you will have many experiences of coitus interruptus and you will get used to pulling on your clothes in a hurry when your little one, who you thought was fast asleep, barges through your door. As your children get older they will become more observant when your nightgown is suddenly inside out or your husband is hidden under a blanket to hide where he has buried his mouth.

So make the most of your freedom. There is life after baby.

There is great sex after baby, too. But it is not as easy and may not be as spontaneous. During pregnancy is the time when you can really appreciate your sex play because you know a change is impending. Don't forget one of the best advantages. You do not need contraception. The horse is already out of the barn. You can really have some fun.

Good sex during pregnancy is going to anchor your relationship. It will give you a solid foundation for the family house you are building together. Have fun and celebrate your pregnancy with abandon.

But what if we are just not in the mood? Will our relationship fall apart?

Don't worry if you are not always in the mood for lovemaking. There is a lot more to sexual connection than intercourse. The idea is to stay connected and to maintain your image of each other as lovers. If you *never* feel in the mood, you definitely want to look into the possible reasons why. But loving each other's bodies and engaging in perpetual foreplay without actual sexual contact can go a long way toward keeping you in each other's sexual sphere.

Nothing is more loving than cuddling with each other, naked or not, while waiting for the baby to kick. When you put your hands on the tummy and feel that recognizable foot or elbow during the latter stages of pregnancy, you will feel elated and close to each other.

Light massage, a kiss behind the ear, or even a whisper can lead to lovemaking. But these gestures are wonderful even if they don't lead anywhere. If you don't want to make love you can use this time to hold each other and bond in many ways.

During the next nine months at least one of you is not going to feel much like experiencing too much nightlife. I would be very surprised to see a perpetual pregnant party animal. Alcohol is a big no-no, so aside from cultural activities and movies you might find many opportunities for quiet activities. A cozy fire, soft music, and some massage oil would be a nice touch.

Pregnancy is not an illness as the Victorians used to think. Women do not need to spend the day in bed resting like little flowers. In fact, historically, with the exception of the rich, most women in "the olden days" worked hard right up to delivery. In some cultures women work, have a baby, and go right back to work with the baby on their backs. But you can spend the day in bed if you want to, which could be a lot of fun.

Women appreciate the willingness of their spouse to be in tune with their shifting needs. Taking things more slowly to determine how your wife is feeling at any given time will ensure that you will have lots of fun when your wife is in the mood. Women like to be treated in a gentle, loving way. When you make love, take your time. Taking your time is good advice whether you are having sex during pregnancy or stealing private time after the baby is born. There are several techniques to enhance your pleasure and your sexual connection whether you are pregnant or not— techniques that I hope you will incorporate into your sex life along with your own discoveries.

Why is sex so important? Aren't there other ways a man and woman should relate?

Sex is the language of lovers. Without it a man and a woman are better off friends. When sex is confined to a monogamous relationship it is like emotional and physical glue. It creates an energy connection that exists whether a couple is together or apart.

Many people are happy with recreational sex. Even in the context of marriage I highly recommend sex for the simple purpose of fun and release. However, sex within marriage serves a higher purpose. It is an important activity that should take priority on any couple's "to-do" list. It is not something that should be relegated behind work, lawn maintenance, and soccer practice. Men and women are supposed to bond with one another through the merging of their bodies. If we were simply meant to procreate, we would not live our lives through the lens of lust.

If you examine most marriages that do not work, you will see that the problems relate to sex and connection. Without sex a couple cannot hope to have true intimacy. Intimate sex requires that you open up and trust another person. If you are unable to do that, you are missing a big element of what makes a good relationship so satisfying.

But like anything else, a good sex life does not come without some effort. There are techniques involved. In my opinion, it would be great if every couple were required to go to sex school before engaging in a committed relationship. Couples often do not have the knowledge to please each other and do not know enough of what pleases them as individuals. We, as a society, tend not to encourage and support couples talking about sex openly, even with each other.

Sex is all around us but for some reason open discussion of healthy sexuality is taboo. Talk shows are filled with aberrant sexual oddities, but women are not confident enough to tell their husbands how they would like to be pleased.

So where do people learn about sex? Kids learn at school and spend years with misinformation. Parents educate their kids about why they shouldn't have sex, or maybe how things work from a mechanical perspective, but rarely explain how to make their sexual lives ultimately fulfilling. They might find this type of discussion to be inappropriate, but at least in the old days parents had the "sex talk" on the wedding day. Now it is assumed that people who might have been sexually active are also sexually educated.

Where do men learn about sex? If they move beyond what they learn in school and from their locker room or football buddies, they are probably learning from watching porno films. Many of the things that these films portray aren't even physically possible, let alone viable, in a true sexual relationship. Pornographic sex does nothing to bring a couple in to an intimate connection.

Where do women learn about sex? Though more women today watch pornos than they will admit—which means they, too, are misinformed—they learn a romanticized perspective of sex from the media and the wealth of steamy romance novels. The so-called chick flicks promote a romanticized view of relationships that leaves a majority of women thinking they are missing out on something.

Women may learn about sex from one another, but with the exception of some currently popular television shows, women have been reluctant to talk openly with each other about sex. They especially do not talk about sexual problems.

If women are relying on the media or erotic depictions in romance novels for their sex information, how can they be anything but misinformed? We send women double messages. Our media enforces the image of women as either sexual or maternal. Good girls or bad girls. Aside from internal conflict about our sexual needs as women, what man can possibly live up to the erotic heroes of our imaginings? Our expectations become widely disproportionate to our realities. We are perpetually disappointed in how we are treated in our relationships, and because of what we expect, we wait for our mates to figure things out on their own.

Sex is communication and requires communication. As a couple you need to set goals just as you would for any other venture. This may sound silly at first, but as you learn to talk about sex and you learn to lovingly communicate your needs, you will be able to get to know what each of you wants and expects from your sexual relationship. For example, if one of you is uncomfortable with oral sex, you need to be able to communicate that to your spouse. Perhaps the problem is that you are not comfortable with your technique. You may feel insecure in your ability to please your mate. Communicate your feelings—the resolution may be as simple as a little lesson in loving.

People are under the misconception that we are naturally going to know how to have sex just because we do it frequently. Your desire to know more about having sex during pregnancy has given you the added benefit of learning how to have better sex at any stage in your relationship. The more you have sex, the more you will have sex. The more you communicate about sex, the better sex you will have.

Sex is important. Satisfying sex is even more important. Sex as a major element of your relationship is important to intimacy. Communication about sex is vital to your level of intimacy. In a good marriage, you hope for friendship and mutual respect, but if you have these elements without the element of sex, your relationship will stagnate and die. It is the difference between *loving* someone and being *in love* with someone. Love without lust is as empty as lust without love. You can raise a child with a friend, but your relationship will be skating on precariously thin ice. Your baby can seal your relationship as a family, but sex will seal your relationship as lovers. It is good to have it all if you want to traverse the terrain of raising a child together without too many spills.

I believe that too many people are in denial about their needs. Whether we are socialized this way or we are responding to our own issues, I can't count how many times I have heard people say, "Well, sex is not the most important thing in the relationship." If so, why are there sexologists like me? When people downplay the importance of sex in their relationship it is because they are probably not getting enough, not getting any, or not getting good sex. There is no honor in not needing sex. You may as well brag about how you don't need air.

When you become parents together you are going to need to put effort into keeping your embers burning. Otherwise you are going to become bored not only with your relationship, but with your life. We can all get involved with work, friends, causes, and dreams, but connection is what we all need the most. Good sex with someone you love means good connection and intimacy. It also takes less work. Enjoying what you have with someone you love takes a lot less work than finding and starting over with someone new.

Why is sex more challenging and perhaps more important for a pregnant couple?

I assume that by the fact that you are reading this you have love and intimacy as your ultimate goal. If you start out on this track now, you are going to be very happy well into your future. I also assume that you probably like sex a lot and want to keep it that way. It is great that you already like sex with each other but I want to make sure that life does not get in the way of your sexual enthusiasm. Call this "prophylactic planning."

Sex is important to pregnant couples because you ideally want to stay together to raise your child. It doesn't happen that way for many people; divorce is far more the norm than otherwise. This is a sad statistic because divorce complicates a child's life, which is complicated enough. It also complicates your future relationships. It is certainly better to do as much as you can to bring your relationship closer together rather than letting it fall apart for lack of planning and emotional investment.

Having a baby is a big and important step for any person. It is a lifelong commitment. Even if you do it badly, you are still going to be doing it, whether you feel up to it or not.

As a pregnant couple you are faced with a major life change. You are both filled with fears and questions. Having a baby together creates an automatic partnership that can help both of you cope with the changes if you work together and not against one another.

This is the opportunity to learn about each other in a natural way and to cross emotional barriers with patience and exploration.

What are some of these emotional issues? If you know what they are you can prevent them from eclipsing your lovemaking and intimacy during your pregnancy and beyond.

Here are some of the most common problems:

- different and often incompatible views of the pregnancy
- disagreement over the man's role in the pregnancy
- differences in attitudes about sex
- resentment over lost youth and freedom
- different views on child rearing
- financial woes

Different and Often Incompatible Views of the Pregnancy

Be honest. You are reading this book, but is it possible that one of you wanted a baby more than the other? People are ready to have children at different stages in their lives. Readiness for one person may not be compatible with the goals of another. Perhaps your original agreement was that you would wait to have children or would not have them at all. If you have an "oops" you are going to have some hidden resentments to deal with.

Contrary to a prevailing cynicism about women and our motives an "oops" can really be an "oops" and not a feminine manipulation. People automatically assume that the woman will want a child before her husband. There are many women who are not elated when they find out they are pregnant. They may be in a loving relationship with their spouse but may not want to get off their career path at a time when things are seemingly prosperous. Or perhaps she is not relishing the idea of losing her figure for nine months, or forever. Not all women are concerned about their "biological clock." Some women would like to throw the clock out of the window forever.

My point is that if the two future parents didn't equally want the baby at this time in their relationship, or were not ready to become parents, it is possible that their intimacy could suffer and that their relationship could be damaged.

Men and women have differing views of pregnancy stemming from generations of familial and cultural influence. We are all affected by what we see and hear throughout our lifetimes. In previous generations, women who were pregnant stayed home and nested, and they continued to stay home after the baby was born. Today, many women work until delivery and return after a short maternity leave.

Some women see their pregnancy as a change in roles. They may see their husbands not as playmates but as protectors.

Men also take on this self-concept as protector. It is not a bad thing, but it is just an additional stress if he is not able to express his concerns.

Both men and women have to accept that they will no longer be the center of their lover's universe. Either of them might feel resentment over the pregnancy even if it was planned, and they might harbor guilt over what is truly a natural response to a major life change.

Disagreement Over the Man's Role in the Pregnancy

Another emotional issue that can be brought into the pregnant bedroom is determining what is expected of the husband during the process. Several factors can spell trouble. Some women have expectations that their husbands will be completely involved every step of the way. This can be dangerous because expectations are a setup for disappointment. You may assume that your husband will want to know every gory detail of your pregnancy at every moment. It does not mean your husband doesn't love you or the baby if he does not want to know every little detail. You can be intimate with someone and still not want them to be involved in every moment of your life.

Don't gauge your joy over your pregnancy by whether or not your husband frames your baby's ultrasound photo and puts it on his desk. Not all men enjoy that kind of thing. It does not mean he is not happy about becoming a father. He may simply be preoccupied with his own anxieties.

Some husbands will want to be involved, or even overinvolved, with the pregnancy every step of the way. Some mothers-to-be do not want to share every one of their special moments during their nine months. Some women feel most womanly when they are pregnant and may be completely immersed in becoming an Earth Mother goddess. While it is not a good idea to cut her husband out completely, it is understandable that a woman would want to revel in her own miracle of creation. Some women despise the nine months of pregnancy, but most of the women I have interviewed say it is one of the best times of their lives.

Differing views of a man's role during the pregnancy can create emotional issues if the feelings are not expressed. A man who feels "put out to pasture" after he makes his sperm contribution is not likely to want to be an involved father after the baby is born. It is important to resolve these role conflicts at an early stage.

Many men are scared during the months of pregnancy because of their impending role as father. If they feel that they are not welcomed into the process, they will be apt to fall into the avoidance category. It is not as easy for the one who is not physically carrying the baby to be as intimately connected. This is why emotional issues regarding the man's role in the pregnancy, and ultimately in fatherhood, will arise.

Differences in Attitudes about Sex

Attitudes about sex create major emotional issues that wind up in the pregnant couple's bedroom. Before we consider actual disagreements, such as when and how much sex during pregnancy, we should look at what emotional issues about sex bring into any relationship.

If we simply look at how women are socialized regarding sex, it is obvious why there are issues of trust and intimacy in marital relationships. Before the sexual revolution women spent so much time saying "no" to protect their reputations that it must have been difficult to be allowed to say "yes." It is an entirely different mentality to see men as shared lovers rather than predators.

It is not much different for women now, even after the changes in acceptable sexual conduct. More people are "doing it" with more people, but ideas about sexual conduct have not changed a whole lot within the general population. Women are making bold choices in experiencing their sexuality outside of marriage, but there is still an attitude about what is bad and what is good. Just because a woman gets married does not mean that she is not going to hold back that part of herself that has been a protection.

Women create sexual walls to avoid being hurt. When they are in a committed marital relationship, they do not easily shed that need for emotional self-protection. Our current generation has more freedom than in years past, but this is also perceived by women as less of a guarantee that she will be cared for or that she won't be abandoned. It is inevitable that these emotional issues will surface in the relationship.

Many men have issues about sex regarding women as lovers or looking at their lover as the mother of their child. Men are also confused about seeing their wives as sexual when they also see them as maternal. There will be a change in how he perceives his wife emotionally and how he perceives her body. All of a sudden she's not his lover anymore and he tends to either start viewing her as a mother, or he views her body as not "his" anymore. It's not "Pleasure Central" anymore. It's a host for this new life and that's the first thing. The immediate change is men tend to become very protective and they will begin viewing the woman as something other than a lover. No man wants to think of himself as having sex with his own mother. And, so, many men will immediately turn off to sex because the woman is pregnant and all of a sudden she's not his lover anymore. She's "a" mother, which is equated with "my" mother, with "you don't have sex with your mother."

Pregnancy brings out many Freudian issues. I think Freud thought too much and should have found a better hobby. It is just like telling someone not to think about something: you know they will. Freud has made all of us think there is something mutually exclusive about sex and motherhood. Just because you find your wife sexy and appealing while she is pregnant does not mean you have some perverse feelings about your mother. This is your wife you are having a baby with, not your mother, so enjoy your wife's juicy and luscious beauty. If you are a breast man you should be in heaven!

It is important to understand that men and women really do differ in their perspective of sex. This is the way human beings were made and there are reasons for it. The sooner men and women give up trying to understand each other, as if we are the same species, the sooner we can go on to the business of happy relationships. Accept the fact that we are built differently and that our brains are not wired the same way.

No matter what that romance novel you have been devouring says, men become romantic and attached to their mate through their penis. Maybe it is because their genitals are "outies," and women's genitals are "innies," but sex is what creates the strongest bond between a man and a woman. Without it men tend to lose their connection. This doesn't mean all men will try to get it somewhere else, but they may find ways to compensate. Have you ever considered why men need testosterone rituals? You don't see too many horny teens who would trade some action for a televised football game with the guys.

By contrast, women create their bond to their husband through their mind. They need to know a man cares deeply about them and will be there to protect them and their children. Women also want to know they are desired and admired. The act of sex is far less important than being appreciated as a woman.

The important point is that both partners in the relationship must own up to their sexual needs and take responsibility for expressing them. Women must accept the fact that when their man complains about not getting enough sex, it is not necessarily true that he sees her only as a sex object. This is his way of maintaining his emotional connection to his mate.

Many couples are consciously or unconsciously at odds about the consistency of their sexual relationship, with one partner (usually the man) seeking sex more frequently. Of course, when they become pregnant and the woman is not able to—or interested in—having intercourse because she feels ill or suffers from a pregnancy-related medical condition, the couple's unstated differences will come quickly to the foreground, potentially causing many problems.

Resentment Over Lost Youth and Freedom

Pregnancy often marks the end of unabridged youth for many couples, as they become "adults" with new responsibilities and concerns. Having a baby is definitely a "spontaneity killer"! Both the man and the woman can have feelings about losing their freedom, and they may blame and resent their partner who "caused this to happen." When a couple announces a pregnancy, everyone's attention automatically shifts to the promise of angelic cherubs. Many couples will ignore their feelings about sex because they are immediately in responsibility mode. They may have many unresolved issues but they think that because they are having a baby, it is too late to address sexual problems that may already exist in their relationship. They may feel pressure to keep up a "good front" in an effort to ensure that their relationship survives for the sake of the baby. They may feel that admitting their feelings or pointing out problems to their mate might jeopardize the relationship and split them apart. Many couples put sex on hold during pregnancy without considering the importance of maintaining sexual connection. They do not consider their many options and are under the false impression that "responsible people" put their own physical needs behind the needs of the developing child. Nine months is a lifetime for a relationship. The habit of putting the needs of the children totally ahead of the needs of the relationship can spell disaster. While lovemaking before children is usually free-flowing and spontaneous, sex and intimacy during pregnancy and after the birth of a child requires planning and effort. If you and your mate are the type of people who view sex as the process of "getting off," you may be having the dinner and missing dessert. If you are only results oriented and look to sex simply as a release, you will be frustrated during this stage of life. There is certainly a lot to be said for the gratuitous orgasm. However, with a little imagination you can be wet, aroused, and preorgasmic any time you choose.

Different Views on Child Rearing

Only after becoming pregnant do many couples begin to think about themselves as parents, only to discover that their respective philosophies on parenting are very different. Whether their disagreements are of major or minor importance, they can generate anger and resentment that can prompt the partners to feel more like enemies than lovers.

Financial Woes

Men become very protective, or at least they should. They become protective not only of her body, but they're all of a sudden her protector; they're the hunter, they're the provider, they're everything, and they feel an overwhelming sense of responsibility and pressure. It can create a lot of stress for a guy. And that's okay. That's normal. These are new roles that both of them are going to have to adjust to.

Having a baby is a serious milestone that forces many couples to take stock of their financial condition. As a result, the couple will often disagree on how to best use their financial resources, or they will begin to worry about not having enough money to support the growing family. Men often feel increased pressure to succeed and to earn more as it is in their inherent nature to protect and provide. And two-partner working couples may begin to worry about what will happen if one partner gives up working to take care of the baby. All in all, money problems are often a huge stumbling block for couples, sabotaging their intimacy unless they learn to cope with the financial anxiety that a new baby will surely bring about.

A lot of women complain when they're pregnant: "He doesn't understand how I feel," blah, blah, blah. We know that he can't because he's not a woman and he doesn't know what it feels like, so it's up to her to tell him. Women, at this point, have to be more vocal and more open to communication than ever before, and to constantly reassure the man. Of course he's going to feel left out! A woman can't just expect a man to automatically know and to automatically have a feeling for what she's going through. It's important that she talk about it.

Dispelling the Myths

Of all the sexual problems that couples worldwide can experience, sex during pregnancy is without a doubt the leading area of misunderstanding and ignorance.

There are emotional issues to overcome when a couple is pregnant, but there are many physical realities as well. Women experience changes in their bodies that are very real. Hormones are very powerful. They can influence mood, physical comfort, internal temperature, and a perspective of reality. This is the time to talk about the changes that you can anticipate and to plan for the changes in a loving, caring way. Lovemaking is a perfect way to maneuver through the potentially rough terrain of changing shape, changing mood, changing tastes, food cravings, and justifiable bitchiness.

Having a good sex life and a foundation for closeness can help diffuse the land mines that are buried beneath a pregnant couple's feet. So as soon as you know the pregnancy test is positive, you can take action and plan for a wonderful experience together.

I loved every second of being pregnant. I felt sexy, loved, and cherished. What was most important for me is that I was very aware of the life growing inside me without losing sight of my sexiness. I love sex. I need it. I have been fortunate that I have learned enough about my own body and about sexuality in my studies that I am able to communicate to my mate what I need to satisfy me. I am also very interested in pleasing my man and keeping the bond strong because I want to be the center of his sexual universe. I have made it my business to know what a man needs and how to heighten his pleasure. Sex is a learned art. This is the time to learn your lessons because it is a change in your relationship. You are facing changes and are raising questions that you might have been able to ignore up until now. This is a perfect opportunity to take Sex 101.

By the time the baby is born you will be a graduate of the school of perpetual bliss.

Use this time to make your marital bed a sanctuary for your life together. This is both a physical bed and a place in your imagination that you can return to when you have a little one to chase around the house. Remember how much of sex is in the mind. If you work together at this stage in your relationship to create the image of the type of sex life you want with each other, you can draw upon this even when opportunity eludes you.

Facing Your Fears

Many myths are associated with pregnancy—especially sex and pregnancy. We will discuss these myths at greater length in the next chapter. At this stage of early pregnancy and throughout the months to follow, it is important for both men and women to confront their innermost fears and insecurities about their relationship.

For example, as a woman's belly grows, so does her fear that her husband will stray. Some women have very good reason to fear this. If a relationship has been built solely on sex for the sake of sex, and not as an expression of intimacy, it is highly possible that the man will consider that his needs are not going to be met by his pregnant wife.

It is sad, but this is a time when a man who is going to stray will find the perfect excuse to do so. This certainly means that the pregnancy has unmasked serious underlying problems in a relationship, but some of these issues can be resolved without stupid choices creating a mess for everyone. It is beneficial to confront the issues directly as they can bring a couple closer instead of destroying their bond.

When a woman becomes pregnant and has unresolved insecurities about the relationship, she may pull away and devote her energy to the process of preparing for motherhood. Very strong mothering instincts should be honored; however, women make the mistake of thinking the process of pregnancy and childbirth is a part of her own inner world. The more a woman leaves her husband out of the process the more she is asking for trouble. If her husband has many insecurities or is immature, he might act out at this time by seeking an affair.

These men may be acting out a refusal to take responsibility for their pending progeny, or they may simply be sexually frustrated because their pregnant wife has not wanted or been able to have sex with them for weeks or months. Their reasoning will justify their choices but the sacred bond will be broken at a time when it is most crucial. It is not worth the agony. Men . . . there is never a good reason to stray during this special and most important time in the life of your marriage. This is a time when your wife needs you the most and you are creating the foundation not only for yourself, but also for your offspring. Think about how important it is for a child to have trust and security. If you can't be trusted during pregnancy, you are setting yourself up for a devastating future. Many people believe that babies are subconsciously aware of the things around them. You do not want your child's first exposure to the world to be filled with guilt or betrayal.

The nine months of pregnancy is a time when couples should try their hardest to communicate about their feelings and to find ways to re-assure each other. Even a trusting relationship can run up against problems of intimacy. It amazes me how difficult it is for couples to discuss issues of romance and sex. We all know what we want but we have trouble expressing it. Many people are too embarrassed or ashamed to talk to their partner; they expect their wife or husband to read their minds.

Many women have told me about frustrating nights when they lie awake watching their satisfied husband sleeping off a good orgasm when they are just getting started. They want to say something but are afraid. They are not even sure what they want to say. This is the situation when there is no pregnancy involved—the communication only becomes more difficult with the proportions of the swelling belly.

The Key to Maintaining a Sexy, Healthy Relationship

As a certified clinical sexologist, I have come to firmly believe that couples must have a deep mutual understanding of their respective sexual needs and drives if they are to remain together in a mutually loving, caring, and compatible relationship.

Keeping intimacy alive throughout pregnancy and after the birth of the child is key to maintaining a healthy, loving, and committed relationship in the future. Having a baby and becoming parents are seldom enough to cause most couples to stay together through difficult times when they are no longer intimate or sexually connected. Don't kid yourself. Sex is important.

Yes, sex is important. How you do it, when you do it, how often you do it is important to the overall health and longevity of your relationship. You go into a marriage wanting it to last. When you prepare to bring a child into the world you are more than likely thinking about raising it together with the one you love. Having a baby is the ultimate intimate act a couple can experience together. Staying sexually connected during and after pregnancy is as important to your relationship as breathing is for staying alive.

Pregnancy Potholes

As we have already touched upon, there are definite potholes on the pregnant couple's path.

- Pregnant couples tend naturally to have sex less often, so the couple is not able to enjoy each other in the way that they formerly did. If the husband used to view his wife's body as his Pleasure Party Central, he now has to consider that he is sharing it with an interloper.
- Second, the couple probably holds many misconceptions and confusion about sex during pregnancy that prevent them from having intercourse or from engaging in close sexual connection.
- Third, the partners may experience emotional, psychological, or financial problems that create anger and resentment between them. Combined, these factors often mean that the nine months of pregnancy and the first three months—if not more—after childbirth can become a danger zone for the couple rather than a period of joy, magic, and enchantment.

No one chooses to be miserable. Even though these potholes can be "typical," they do not have to be the norm. While you are navigating these potholes you can view this time as a "bridge"—to a new and better intimate sexual connection that will take you safely and happily to the next phase of your relationship. Your level of intimacy and your sex life will be altered by having children. I wouldn't attempt to tell you otherwise. But these changes can certainly be for the better.

If the pregnant one is not feeling up to having sex during certain phases of her pregnancy, attitude, teasing, and the promise of fun in the future can go a long way. It is not pleasant to be so tired you can't keep your head off the desk during work, so swollen that your knees feel like water balloons, so nauseated that you feel perpetually seasick, and so huge that you can't even pick yourself up out of a chair. Loving touches, soft caresses, and a sense of appreciation go a very long way and can spell many future "paybacks" for the wise and caring husband. There are days when pregnant women feel great and more "hot to trot" than ever. Timing is everything.

Sexual connection does not only mean intercourse and orgasm. It is the perception of yourselves as lovers first and foremost. Becoming parents is part of the intimate role a couple can play together. The divorce rate is ridiculously high. The imbalance between parenting, marriage partnership, and intimacy is a major cause. If you focus on your baby to the detriment of your relationship, you are making things worse. A child would prefer a healthy relationship between parents who love each other than two divorced parents who indulge him. Now is the time to do some relationship vaccination. Intimate and satisfying sex is the best cement a relationship can have.

I don't believe that lust is the basis of any relationship except one that is purely for recreation. What I mean is that a couple who is in love needs to connect on a physical level to maintain an emotional bond. Sex is an expression of love. Whether it is playful, lusty, or profound, it creates a bond that can help couples work through the inevitable challenges of life.

Keeping It Hot When a Baby Is on the Way

Pregnant couples have some unique challenges. Aside from the myths and misinformation, which we will discuss further in the next chapter, it can be difficult to maintain a sexual connection when the man refuses to listen to his penis and the woman doesn't believe that she is sexy.

If a man is afraid to have a sexual relationship with his pregnant wife or is having his libido drowned in a sea of worry and anxiety, he may need a little help. His wife may need to remind him and his "friend" that there is a reward at the end of the tunnel. It is important for the mother-to-be to reassure her mate that she is interested in having sex and that it is okay to do so, even though her body has a new purpose. Now it's the host for a new life, which for many women can make them feel very sexy. It's very powerful and all of a sudden they say, "Hey, wow, my body's going to produce a new life and it's the joining of the love between—hopefully the love between—myself and my significant other," and it adds to their sensation of pleasure. So, a lot of times what you have is a man who pulls away and a woman who wants it more.

I hear complaints from many women that "My husband doesn't ever start anything with me, I have to be the one." This is not a problem, ladies, it is a benefit. I, personally, like the power I wield over the family jewels. Give up the dream of being swept off your feet and take charge of having it when you want it and how you want it. It doesn't take much to convince a man that sex is not only a good idea but that it was his idea in the first place. Don't sit and wait for action. Make it happen. You want your man to want you. It is a sure way to keep harmony in your home. This may sound archaic, but it really works. It is not that complicated.

As for you husbands, you need to be extra gentle with your wife's ego. Never, never comment on her size. Relish her femininity and never miss an opportunity to tell her so. Pregnancy is only nine months but it can seem like an eternity if your wife decides she is too unattractive to put out. Know that the woman is already anticipating losing her figure, she's probably already feeling sick, and her body is about to take a different form. She's feeling the chemical changes between the cravings, the nausea, the breast tenderness, the headaches, lower back pain, and so on. She may be having some unusual vaginal discharge or vaginal odor, so already she's feeling potentially uneasy about her body. It's very important that the man reassure her that she's sexier to him than ever, especially if he wants to make love. Really stress the fact that her new body turns you on.

It is not nice to make your wife feel unattractive even if you are the type of man who is not wise enough to see the ultrasexiness of a woman with child. Similarly, men must understand that if their woman declines interest in sex during pregnancy, it does not give him license to have sex with another woman. Instead, he needs to recognize that she may be signaling to him that she needs protection, comfort, and stability before she is ready for sex.

Society has conditioned us to think of pregnancy as a feminine affliction . . .

To keep things hot during pregnancy, you might have to plan. But planning and making some extra effort are not necessarily bad things. For example:

• You wake up feeling queasy. You reach for the soda crackers permanently placed by your bedside and shove some in your mouth like a cork. It doesn't help. For the past two months you have started your morning with a new ritual. Open eyes, feel queasy, reach for the crackers, run to the bathroom, slide into position over the porcelain god, and barf out your crackers before you even have a chance to swallow them.

• You drag yourself back into bed and stop yourself from flattening your husband's head with the phone. Instead you admire the curve of his back peering from behind a carelessly strewn blanket.

• He feels you and rolls over with a smile. You try to forget the taste in your mouth that even toothpaste can't erase. He has the look of mischief but just when you think you might be up for some fun, a second wave hits you and you begin the process again.

This is a perfect example when some tentative planning might be in order. Your husband, sensing that he almost got the phone on the head for causing this condition, provides you with some much needed sympathy. He tells you he will try to slip away from the office during lunch to see if you are feeling better.

You know what he means. You hope that your nausea subsides as it typically does after breakfast. You feel excited thinking about your date. You know that your husband is going to come home for the specific purpose of making love to you. This is sexy. You take a shower and slather yourself with sweet-smelling lotion and wait for your lover to return.

This is what a little patience and planning can do for you. It takes effort and understanding, but you may find that you like this kind of special date long after your baby is driving a car. When a couple plans an off-schedule yet specific time to be alone, there is more of a sense of concentration on each other. So much of sex is experienced between commercials. When you are forced to plan to stay connected you may have a better quality experience even if the sex is less frequent and spontaneous.

When you have a plan, you build up desire. You create focus. You may not be able to have a quickie anywhere or at any time that you would like, but when you do make love, you can bet that you will appreciate your time together. Especially if you do it right. Now don't get ahead of yourself. We'll get to the doing . . . I promise.

What You Think You Know about Pregnancy Might Put a Damper on Your Sex Life

As you know, couples typically think that their sex life has to change when the couple is pregnant. Even though there are reasons you might abstain or avoid as we have already touched upon, you do not have to reduce the frequency or, for the most part, the positions or practices that you are used to. Unless her doctor has told a woman that she does have to abstain from or modify her sexual practices, sex can continue the way that it was before the pregnancy. Believe it or not, many men will avoid sex while the woman is pregnant because they're afraid they're going to hurt the baby.

On the other hand, after a baby is born everything is not going to be the same as it was pre-pregnancy. Different doesn't mean bad. But husbands in particular should not expect everything to go back to "normal" immediately. The biggest damage is done when there is not an awareness of the change in roles or the pending change in roles and all of a sudden it's upon you and you don't understand why you're having these sudden conflicts, these sudden feelings. First of all it's important to know that the roles will change and certain things come along with that. Certain biological changes, physical changes, are unavoidable, but if you're aware of them you can work with them.

*   *   *

Some women will join the men in the camp "Oh, my God, I can't have sex anymore. I have to radically alter everything that I'm doing, and, you know, I could have a miscarriage. I don't want his penis in me anymore. I don't want to have orgasms anymore."

Oftentimes, too, I've talked to many women who suddenly become very prudish and almost return to virginity when they become pregnant, because now it's the same—it's the perception of role change. You know, "I'm not your lover anymore. I'm going to be a mother and a mother behaves like *this*." And it depends on what culture or what religion they've been brought up in. Some women return to purity or prudishness. "Get away from me. I need to protect this new life inside me." And, "Okay, your work is done now." Often women who are pregnant for the first time tend to take the protective stance. Women who've had a baby before understand that no harm's going to come to the baby; they tend to take on the goddess role.

Couples who disagree on the type and frequency of sex during pregnancy or after birth, and who let their sexual bond dissipate over time, are likely to encounter further problems that tend to cause one or both partners to become sexually "disenfranchised."

In short, pregnancy and the transition to parenthood can be a minefield for many couples. One-third of all separations and divorces occur within three years of having a baby. Is this a coincidence? Probably not. It is a strong confirmation that pregnancy and parenthood introduce conflicts so severe that millions of marriages do not survive them.

All throughout your pregnancy you have found ways to show each other your desire and love. Your husband has made a habit of rubbing your tummy with natural oil. He rubs it all around your hips and thighs and gently between your legs into the fine tufts of hair surrounding your pleasure spot. You are most comfortable on your side but sometimes he sits behind you and rubs his chest against your back and gently kisses your neck. You are relaxed and aroused and he leads you to the edge of the bed where he guides your head to a pillow he has set out for you. He rubs your shoulders and moves his hands down your back to your buttocks. He rubs the remaining oil on his hands on your round curves and enters your vagina from behind. You are filled with his warmth as he rubs against the sides of your swollen crevasses. You sway forward and back until you reach your peak. You feel him tense and release with your pleasure wave. Something is different. You are not just playing. You are sharing and connecting. You are thinking of nothing but each other, not work, not the bills, not the baby. He senses it too. You cuddle up to each other under the covers and feel the energy between you. You know that your intimate love-making has helped you feel him with you even when he is not there.

Don't worry if you are not there yet. You have just begun reading this book. But this is where you want to be. While you are pregnant together you can build the closeness that you will carry with you throughout your life together. Today you share the joining of your bodies in the cre-ation of new life. After the baby is born you will still be joined by your love and your connection. This is what pregnant sex is all about.

Chapter Two

Myths and Misinformation

When you form a relationship with someone you create an impression based on many characteristics. You know what that person looks like, you know what you feel like around him, and you know certain things about your compatibility. A lot of what you believe about the person you love is based on observation and assumption. You don't really know what is in his mind unless he tells you, and you certainly are not privy to all of the thoughts and feelings that lurk in the farthest recesses of our psyches.

When you make love to your mate, the same is true. You know how you feel together and you know certain things by the responses you share. You know that some things work better than others. You also know that some things make you feel closer while some things keep you apart.

All human beings bring issues into the bedroom that they may never share. Many of these thoughts, feelings, fears, and misconceptions are often not even close enough to the surface to be understood. I wouldn't be a sexologist if people did not have hang-ups about sex. There would be no need for most forms of therapy if sex were a subject that could be dealt with in the open without fear of reprisal. As a society we are more inclined to focus on deviance rather than what can make sexuality a safe and healthy sharing between lovers.

Add to this the element of pregnancy and you have a perfect opportunity for conflict and misunderstanding. You have learned in Chapter One that sex is important to intimacy. You quite probably are convinced that sex during pregnancy is a wonderful idea and you agree that connection is a good thing to have in a long-term loving relationship.

We enter into this subject in agreement that it is a good idea to maintain a sex life during this very special time; however, we have not resolved the problem of what you bring into the bedroom with you. When you are more casual about sex, these fears and misconceptions seem not to take such a front seat. If you are finding pleasure in your sexual contact, there is no reason to go any further in analyzing it. If it is good, don't mess with it.

However, now you are pregnant and you are looking at everything differently. We have talked about roadblocks to intimacy for pregnant couples. Now we can see more closely how misinformation and fear can influence how you relate to each other during this time.

Pregnancy has always been a mystery to humankind. In the days of the cave people, it is likely they had no sense of connection between the act of sex and the arrival of offspring. Throughout history there have been many theories about how conception occurs. They sound amusing and a bit ridiculous today, but in a few hundred years some of our beliefs may give future sexologists, if they need to exist at all, reasons to giggle as well.

In all fairness to our attempts at sophistication and understanding of how things work, if you consider the mystery and confusion that has surrounded pregnancy since the beginning of time, it's no wonder that we still have some pervasive myths. Oh, if you still believe in some of these myths, don't let me stop you. Myths passed down from generation to generation are sometimes the hardest to dispel.

Throughout the ages, myths associated with sex and pregnancy tended to fall into two major categories: those based on fear, and those based on hope. Thinking that you can't have sex while you're pregnant, or that your husband's penis can hurt the baby, are myths based on fear (unless you have a high-risk condition that warrants abstaining from intercourse or orgasm). The idea that your sex life will go back to being exactly what it was before pregnancy and the arrival of your baby is definitely based on hope. But of course that is why you are reading this. As you already know, although things will be different, you will probably have a better sex life than before, when you combine new information with an active effort to keep things hot and sexy between you.

The next section of the book takes you through the three trimesters of pregnancy. You will be making some modifications according to what is happening in the mother's body. What you may not realize is that you will also be making modifications in light of the preconceived notions and fears that you bring to the pregnancy.

By and large, for the first trimester, unless you have a history of miscarriage or have been advised otherwise, you can continue to enjoy the sex life you have been enjoying all along. You may see that you have had some issues with sex or some major inhibitions before you were pregnant. But this is the time when you can bring these things to the surface and discuss them lovingly so you can work them through together.

Concerns that are particular to pregnancy can get in the way of your normal sex life. Even if you are told by a doctor or by a book that it is okay for you to continue to have an active sex life, you may find this hard to believe. Many couples harbor anxiety or a sense of intangible fear that if they continue having sex while pregnant, something "bad" will happen.

If you're feeling a little like that yourself, it's completely understandable. After all, up until about twenty years ago, doctors were still advising women not to have "sexual relations" during the first trimester, for fear of miscarriage, or during the last trimester, for fear of inducing premature labor. Of course, we now know that in a healthy pregnancy sex does not bring on miscarriage or labor, but old ideas die hard. Many of our mothers and grandmothers were no doubt instructed to avoid or abstain from sex during their pregnancies.

Be very aware that the second you announce a pregnancy you will get a lot of well-meaning advice that will probably scare you. Every woman who has ever had a baby has a story to tell. The problem is that many of the people giving you advice had their babies long before you were born.

Ideas and medical facts change all of the time. What might have been the thinking of the day is likely to be very different in the next generation. Many things that have not changed have been found to be better than the way we do things now. But unfounded archaic myths that generate fear should be confronted and dismissed.

Certainly, as you read on through this chapter and hear some of the myths from the Middle Ages and even the late 1800s, you'll be glad that you live now. We may still be ignorant about certain things but at least we are not bizarre. If you can imagine what the world was like during these time periods, it is not hard to see why these particular beliefs prevailed. Keep in mind, however, that some of this misinformation formed the basis of some of the myths that confound us today.

Dispelling the Myths

Here are a few common myths as seen from the perspectives of the woman and the man.

Many Pregnant Females Believe:

- Lovemaking is forbidden for the rest of the pregnancy because it will hurt the baby.
- My husband shouldn't ejaculate in me because it might cause premature labor.
- I don't look sexy anymore, so I don't want to make love or be intimate.
- I don't look sexy anymore so how can my husband want me?
- Don't touch my breasts because you'll contaminate the milk.
- We can't have sex after the 2nd (or 3rd, 4th, 5th, 6th, 7th, 8th, 9th, depending on the myth) month.
- I can't masturbate because it might harm the baby.
- I can't have an orgasm because it will bring on labor.

Male Myths:

- I'm afraid to put my penis in since the baby might feel or see it.
- I'm afraid to ejaculate in you because the semen might cause birth defects.
- Sweetheart, you can give me pleasure, but there's nothing I can do for you.
- Since we can't have intercourse, we can't have sex.

- I know you don't feel well, so it's probably better if I don't ask you for sex for nine months.
- I'm entitled to have sex with another woman because you can't meet my sexual needs.
- Our sex is boring now, because there's only one position we can make love in.
- The baby was just born, so now we can resume our usual sex life.

Most of these myths come from the same root: there is something unsafe or unsanitary about having sex during pregnancy. Modern medicine gives no credence to these fears unless there is a specific medical reason to support them. Try not to get caught up in these anxieties. If you keep them to yourself, you won't understand why your lover is behaving hesitant or withdrawing from you. Remember to reassure each other.

If you listen to these myths early on, the man will feel forsaken and the woman will feel rejected. This is not a good way to start your new life together. Get over your fears. Ask questions. If you don't believe what you read in these pages, get a second opinion from your doctor. Better yet, listen to your own bodies. Follow the rhythms of your own bodies and your desire for each other. Communicate, communicate, communicate. See the situation from the perspective of your spouse. You want to sustain your intimate connection in any way you can. It can be a positive experience to explore your fears and the validity of these myths together. But don't avoid each other and don't avoid sex. You will not be happy. It will be a very long nine months.

So where did all of these myths originate and how have they changed throughout history? There have always been great mysteries in life that we mere mortals have tried to explain away with our efforts at logic and primitive science. Sometimes we just guess. We interpret what we see even if it is not always accurate. Look how long it took for people to realize that germs were a cause of disease.

Let's keep an open mind. With certain data we might have thought the same things under the same circumstances. For now, let's take a sweeping tour of some of the myths that have abounded throughout recorded history.

The Art of Getting Pregnant

Conception has always been a wellspring for popular myth. Once it was clearly determined that there was a correlation between intercourse and having babies, people tried to control the outcome with homespun fertility secrets.

You could count on having a baby if you:

- Lay a baby on your bed.
- Douche with apple cider.
- Swallow a watermelon seed.
- Let the light of a full moon shine on your belly.

Many of these superstitions still circulate today. Some of them might actually work.

What we do know for sure is that for conception and birth to occur a man's sperm cell and a woman's egg cell have to meet; stay together long enough for fertilization to occur; travel to their new home in the womb; subdivide, grow, and develop for nine months; and then make their grand entrance. We also know that the sperm cell is what dictates the sex of the baby. This may seem like a small bit of information, but the lack of this information was the cause of much controversy and suffering. In fact, in addition to wreaking havoc in the lives of women who were cast aside for bearing only girls, this ignorance played a significant part in the rift that occurred between the Catholic Church and Henry VIII, King of England in the 1500s.

When Henry's first wife, Catherine, failed to produce a male successor to the throne, he decided to use this affront to ask the church to annul the marriage. His ulterior motive was to be free to marry Anne Boleyn, with whom he had reportedly fallen in love. When Pope Clement VII would not grant Henry's request, King Henry VIII obtained a divorce through Thomas Cranmer, whom he had made archbishop of Canterbury. At that point, all ties that bound the English church to Rome were shattered, and the pope's authority in England was abolished. When Henry's second wife, Anne Boleyn, did not eventually give birth to a boy and he tired of her, she was put to death. History could have been altered if Henry had known that it was his sperm that was being obstinate. Because of his sperm, the pope lost authority over England and Anne Boleyn lost her head. But Henry never would have admitted that he was so myth-taken.

Hippocrates, the father of medicine, had a sense that a fetus was the fruit that grew as a result of the joining of the female and male seeds. This was pretty close and we can give him an "A" for effort. Aristotle, however, proclaimed, "The woman functions only as a receptacle, the child being formed exclusively by means of the sperm." That is a little too self-serving for my taste.

Meanwhile, ancient doctors had countless recommendations for enhancing fertility.

Fertility Recommendations for Men Included:

- Eat plenty of fennel, a vegetable reputed to make men more virile. (There's no evidence that this works, but it may have made their breath smell good enough for sex to be a possibility!)
- Do not ejaculate too often, or the sperm will be diluted.

Fertility Recommendations for Women Included:

- Drink the saliva of lambs (I wonder how they collected it?).
- Drink a broth made from the dried and ground up womb of a rabbit or hare.
- Wear earthworms tied to a chain or rope around your neck.

As for prime positions for conception, the poet Lucretius said, "It seems clear that the female is most readily impregnated in the posture of the four-footed animals."

Once the deed is done, the advice becomes even more creative. Soranus of Ephesus, considered the father of gynecology, said that if a woman wanted to conceive, after she had intercourse, she was to massage her stomach with the oil of fresh green olives and refrain from bathing for seven days. She was also cautioned against rocking in a chair. Other doctors told women to remain lying down and keep their legs tightly crossed. The length of time they were to do this seemed to have a wide range from a few minutes to the rest of the night.

Meanwhile, the medieval church permitted only one position for conception, the man and woman facing each other. There appears to have been a special dispensation granted for people who were too obese to do it this way; basically, they were permitted to do it any which way they could. I wonder how the Church knew what was going on behind closed doors?

Once a woman had missed her "menses," Pliny the Elder suggested that in order to ward off miscarriage, she should drink a concoction made from the ashes of a porcupine and apply a light ointment, made from hedgehog fat, on her belly.

Perhaps some of the greatest controversies concerning conception were focused on the question of a woman's pleasure. Throughout history influential sages seem to have been divided on this one. Some thought a woman had to enjoy sex in order to conceive and to have a well-formed baby. Others thought that if she was experiencing pleasure during the act of conception she was defiling the pure spirit of the baby and could give birth to an evil or demonic child. Think of all the repression and hang-ups that one created.

In the thirteenth century, Saint Thomas Aquinas condemned the idea of a woman actually enjoying intercourse. Some theologians agreed, however, with the idea that a woman's pleasure played a role in the beauty of the baby. As if that debate wasn't hot enough, others joined in and asserted that if a woman repressed her enjoyment, it was because she was trying not to conceive, which was considered a sin. Later in the same century, men were advised to prolong their lovemaking until their wives climaxed. This, they were assured, would give the best chance of producing a healthy, aesthetically pleasing baby. Of course necessity is the mother of invention. If the climax was too elusive, these men had to resort to some creative thinking. Some were even known to encourage their wives to fondle themselves to achieve orgasm.

When You're "With Child"

Once a woman was "with child," guidance and advice ran the gamut. Some doctors today hold on to the outdated advice that pregnant women should limit the frequency of sexual intercourse during the pregnancy, avoid swimming and other athletic activities, and "eat for two."

You already know what I think and know about having sexual intercourse during pregnancy. Yes, yess, yesssssssss! As for the other admonitions, swimming is actually fine, so long as you know how to swim, use common safety sense, and the water is not too cold and not too hot. Hot tubs are best avoided not only for the baby but for you as well. Physical exercise is encouraged during pregnancy according to the level of activity you maintained prior to becoming pregnant. There are certain types of exercises you can do even if you have never done anything, especially stretching, but it is best to check with a doctor who is knowledgeable about such things.

Watch out for doctors who tell you to eat for two. I would doubt that you would find one, as much as you would like to be given the permission to overindulge. Moderation is the key and a doctor who would tell you to eat in an unhealthy way is ignorant of the relationship between good nutrition and a healthy pregnancy. Surprisingly enough, many doctors do not place a priority on nutrition in their practices. Nutrition is only now being considered more seriously in many medical practices. You may need to educate yourself about good nutrition, but remember that while you need more food during pregnancy, gorging is strictly for your own recreation.

Even though some practitioners have not caught up with times at least pregnant women are not feared as they were in the Middle Ages. In the Middle Ages the bellies of pregnant women were thought to be filled with mysteries and possibly magic. Pregnancy was also considered to be a sort of illness, especially if a woman was thought to be carrying a girl.

In the seventeenth century, pregnant women were routinely bled and purged. I find this particularly hard to imagine, but these treatments were in vogue during that time period and some families begged, borrowed, and stole in order to afford them. The experts of the day varied considerably on prescriptions for how often a woman should be bled.

They also considered how frequently, if ever, a woman was permitted to dance. Nearly all doctors at this time agreed on one thing: Women should absolutely abstain from sexual intercourse for the duration of her pregnancy.

One of the few physicians to go against the tide of the seventeenth century was a doctor named Dionis. This insightful man actually went out on a professional and moral limb when he admonished a fellow Doctor Mauriceau for prescribing abstinence. Dionis said, "Mauriceau could not have made these observations at first-hand, having never had a single child in 46 years of marriage. For me, who had a wife who became pregnant 20 times and gave me 20 children that she successfully brought to term, I am persuaded that the husband's caresses spoil nothing." It's been more than two hundred years since Dionis made this assertion, yet people today still worry about having sex during pregnancy. You can see how long it sometimes takes to clear up a misconception!

Misconceptions, superstitions, and frankly what seems like idiocy in hindsight, seemed to be the prevailing theme of pregnancy during the 1700s and well into the 1800s. Some of the most bizarre accounts involved a pregnant woman's cravings. Some doctors and midwives insisted that no matter what a pregnant woman craved, she must indulge herself, or her baby would be deprived of an essential element for its development and would be born with a defect or abnormality. Of course, there were those who scoffed at that line of reasoning, including Jacques Blondel, author of *Dissertation sur la force de l'imagination des femmes enceintes* (Dissertation on the Power of Imagination of Pregnant Women), published in 1788. Blondel wrote, "How can it be conceded that tucked into his womb a fetus could pine after a glass of champagne, a piece of Westphalian ham, or a salmon from Newcastle?"

Blondel may have raised some eyebrows and encouraged some doubt, but a hundred years after his book was published, wild stories supporting the idea that cravings should be satisfied at any cost were still running rampant. In one story, a pregnant woman was overtaken by a desire to bite the shoulder of the local baker. Her husband paid the baker to indulge his wife's craving, and the woman was able to take two bites out of the baker. She craved a third bite, but the man would not let her bite him again for any price. The woman gave birth to triplets and one of them was stillborn. These sorts of stories were the "urban legends" of the time.

While they perpetuated myths and misinformation, they were generally more innocuous than the moral and behavioral doctrines—or dos and don'ts—which were founded in fear and ignorance.

Pregnancy Dos and Don'ts

You only have to go back a couple of generations to find some incredibly stifling pregnancy rules for women. If you look back several generations, or about eighty years, you can easily see where many of today's myths were seeded.

For example, in the nineteenth century, women who were "with child," were not supposed to step foot outside of their homes after sunset. In some communities, once a woman started to "show," it was considered indecent for her to leave her home at all. She was literally in a state of confinement and at the mercy of her husband, family, and neighbors to take care of any responsibility that went beyond the doors of her house. She was also told never to weigh herself, or to even think about the weight she was gaining because this could impair the development and growth of her baby. (I can see where that one could have its advantages!)

Numerous doctors had lists of unfounded "dos and don'ts" throughout the nineteenth century and well into the twentieth century:

- Pregnant women were told not to sing, because the vibration caused by the voice might hurt the child.
- Pregnant women were forbidden to swim, waltz, or even walk quickly.
- Pregnant women were often advised against sitting on swings or rocking chairs, because both of those motions were considered detrimental to the baby.

Ironically, women today are advised to remain physically active and avoid being too sedentary, unless they have certain high risks involved with their health. We also have convincing evidence that shows that both the mother and the baby benefit from harmonious sounds and smooth movement. Today's mothers-to-be are playing classical music to their babies, singing to them, and even reading to them when they're still within the womb. My how times change!

Up until the 1920s, respected medical authorities were still putting swimming and far more innocent activities on the "don't" list. For instance, in 1921, Leon Pouliot in his book, *Hygiene de la maman et de bébé* (Hygiene of the Mother and Child), cautioned women about walking through shops, riding on the streetcar, and even reorganizing their cupboards. Other doctors prohibited using the sewing machine and riding on a bicycle or a horse. Oddly enough, though pregnant women weren't supposed to clean their cabinets, it was okay to have friends over for dinner. "The intimate evening party with friends, ended at an early hour, spent in pleasant conversation or augmented by a round of bridge is perfectly permissible."

Regardless of what the experts agreed or disagreed about, nearly all women in the nineteenth and early twentieth century sought to gain protection for their developing fetuses by wearing religious ribbons or medals; using amulets and magic spells; praying to saints, gods, and goddesses; or making ritualistic offerings. While this may sound just as silly as some of the doctors' ideas, there *is* merit in having hope. Today's community of physicians, therapists, and healers are now showing that hope, belief, and faith are as powerful, and more so in some cases, than many medicines or treatment plans. While I don't recommend blind faith, there's a lot to be said about believing in something that's bigger than we are. All of today's scientists put together can't create a single cell. (Cloning is a far cry from creating.) And yet, essentially, during conception two cells come together and from there an entire human being is structured and formed. No matter how much we learn about the mechanics of pregnancy and childbirth, the mystery of life remains an inspiration.

Giving Birth

While the idea of giving birth at home, without a doctor, might sound frightening or even horrifying to you, for thousands of years that's how it happened. For most women, particularly the poor, there was little pomp and circumstance surrounding this event. They went about their daily lives until their water broke, and would then give birth and be back to work within days or sometimes even hours. However, for well-to-do women—particularly in ancient civilizations—giving birth was treated with a certain amount of luxury and comfort.

In the second century B.C., wealthy Greeks and Romans treated child-birth as a glorious event. They had a special room set aside specifically for childbirth. This room would be richly decorated with purple curtains and bedspreads, which were often fringed in gold. The room typically had a large bed, or two smaller beds, and sometimes an armless chair de-signed for giving birth, called appropriately a birthing chair. When the woman went into labor, a crackling fire would be built in the fireplace of the birthing room and servants would fill the room with fragrant flowers.

A famous doctor during this time, Soranus of Ephesus, recommended that to help nature along the following things were necessary for the process of birth. He suggested that the birthing room be kept ready with olive oil, hot water, hot compresses, soft sponges, raw wool, bandages, a cushion, fragrant products, a birthing chair or an armchair, two beds, and a conveniently furnished room. Though very few women at the time could afford all or even most of these doctor's suggestions, some of his guidance is still applicable today. For example, he suggested that women be comforted with warm hands or cloths soaked in warm oil. Many cou-ples used this advice during the birth process and find that it works very well. Doesn't it sound nice? Why wait until labor?

Pliny the Elder (A.D. 23–79), author of *Natural History,* a veritable treasure chest of scientific information from ancient times, nonetheless gave childbearing women some of the worst advice ever heard. Pliny pre-scribed potions, which included snails, earthworms, and the pulverized droppings of geese.

Unfortunately, childbirth didn't increase very much in comfort or safety between ancient times and the Middle Ages. Ignorance continued to reign, and although there were a few advances made, midwives who gained a reputation for success were few and far between. Today, we sometimes think of midwives as an "alternative" or even "New Age" trend, but they're actually more of a blast from the past. It's only been in the past one hundred to two hundred years that women have been going to a hospital to give birth. Up until the eighteenth century, doctors who were male gave advice about pregnancy, but they did not involve themselves in the childbirth experience. In fact they were actually prohibited from participating.

Male participation in childbirth was a major societal infraction. In the 1560s a doctor in Hamburg, Germany, who attended a birth disguised as a midwife was accused of Satanism, condemned to death, and burned alive. Several years later, in 1573, Ambroise Pare published *De la genera-tion de l'homme et manière d'extraire les enfants du ventre de leur mère* (On the Procreation of Man and Method of Extracting Infants from the Abdomen of Their Mother). The medical community turned its back on Pare, calling his book immoral and an embarrassment to the profession. The *reputable* doctors all agreed that the world of childbirth was not meant for men.

The moral code that banned men from participating in or even witnessing childbirth held firm until about the beginning of the nineteenth century. But even as late as the end of the eighteenth century, numerous doctors condemned their colleagues who entered the realm of childbirth and also cautioned women against allowing doctors to participate in this experience.

For instance, Doctor Philippe Hecquet's book, *De l'indecence aux hommes d'accoucher les femmes* (On the Indecency of Men Attending Women in Childbirth) ridiculed, condemned, and berated physicians who crossed the line of decency by meeting a woman's vagina—up close and personal—to deliver her baby. Even doing it under a sheet was considered taboo, because the man still had to touch the woman's legs and possibly her genital area. This was confirmed by one of the most esteemed doctors at the close of the eighteenth century. Doctor Baudelocque said, "The touch is the most dangerous of all the senses and leads to lubricity. . . . To what dangers do Christians who put themselves in the hands of a doctor expose themselves?"

So during the Middle Ages, the task of bringing babies into the world belonged to older women who had learned what to do from attending and participating in many births over the years. Oftentimes, the skills of the midwife were passed down from mother to daughter. These women knew very little about anatomy, medicine, or the importance of cleanliness. But they did now how to calm the laboring woman, help her to relax, and boost her confidence. Many midwives also had some knowledge of healing herbs that could be taken internally or applied as creams or salves to ease pain or slow bleeding. Many of the potions that were prescribed had little if any medicinal merit, however, other than their possible placebo effect. For instance, to bring on labor or relieve pain, some midwives recommended making a salve of snake fat or the gall of an eel and applying this to the woman's belly. The powered hoof of a donkey or mule, the hide of a rabbit or hare, the skin of a viper, or the tongue of a chameleon could also be made into a salve in order to produce the same effects.

Once the contractions were coming more often and a fire was roaring in the hearth, the midwife or one of the other women neighbors would put a large cauldron filled with water over the fire. The woman's husband would typically be given the job of gathering or chopping wood to keep the fire going, but was otherwise not directly involved unless there was an emergency and his wife or baby was in danger of dying.

Typically, the laboring woman undressed and sat in her bed, propped up by pillows. The delivery was still made without the midwife looking at the exposed mother's genitals. The laboring mother was covered by a sheet and the midwife delivered the baby by relying entirely on her hands to know what was happening under the sheet. (This went on until the nineteenth century.) The mother-to-be was permitted to move around or change position as often as she liked, and some midwives encouraged women in labor to walk back and forth across the room or to climb up and down stairs.

The midwife, along with female relatives and other close neighbors, stayed with the woman throughout labor and delivery, and sometimes for a few days after the baby was born. This group of women provided comfort, knowledge, and experience with childbirth, confidence, stories, and humor. Midwives were usually paid with a chicken, some eggs, or other form of barter, but her "attendants" were all willing volunteers. Although today men are allowed in the delivery room, women still often engage female birth coaches to support them through the delivery.

Doctors were absent from childbirth up until the fifteenth century, and even then were only available to wealthy families—and that was only when serious complications arose.

The attitude of the times was that a woman's body during pregnancy and childbirth was taboo. There was a recognition that the vagina was still an object of sexuality, so there were mixed messages as to whether a woman giving birth was to be considered good or bad.

Two significant changes occurred with childbirth in the sixteenth century. One was that doctors were becoming increasingly involved in childbirth, and the second was the return of the ancient birthing chair. Many midwives owned a birthing chair, and in villages too small to have a midwife, the church or community generally owned one that all of the women could use. During the sixteenth and seventeenth centuries in Holland, the majority of well-to-do women had her own birthing chair. The chair was reputed to be a better option than a bed because it could be easily transported and offered a variety of positions. In some ways, birthing chairs ushered in a new, more medical era of childbirth, in which women were kept still and treated as "ill." The chair gradually led to the invention of a labor bed. Though the labor bed looked like an improvement for women, the reality is that a more upright or squatting position is actually a more natural and conducive position for giving birth. However, in the eighteenth century, obstetricians praised the prone or semiprone position, primarily because this position made it easiest for them. Ironically, these positions later became mandated by leading obstetricians and hospitals and are still being used in hospital delivery rooms today. This is another perfect example of the value in tracing a belief or practice back to its roots.

Though pregnancy was a mystery to our predecessors, childbirth was even more conducive to the prevalence of myths. In ancient times and right up through the eighteenth century, most newborns were almost immediately adorned with a protective charm or stone, most often worn as part of a necklace. Some stones, such as jasper, malachite, and lapis lazuli, were believed to have healing powers, so they were popular choices for "baby stones." Before babies born in ancient Greece or Rome were given a "baby stone," or any close care or attention, they had to be officially accepted by their parents. If the baby was "deformed" or appeared sickly or weak, the parents could legally abandon or kill them.

Incredibly, breast-feeding was another controversy that raged over several centuries, beginning as early as the second century in the empires of Egypt, Rome, and Greece. Women's breasts inspired much heated debate even then. Some things never change!

The early Egyptians nursed their own babies, except for the pharaoh's wife, who employed one or more live-in wet nurses to feed her babies for her. Meanwhile, doctors in Greece and Rome were advising women to hire wet nurses rather than breast-feed their own children. Ironically, one of the biggest reasons doctors gave this advice was based on the claims of none other than Pliny the Elder (the same guy who told pregnant women to eat geese droppings). According to Pliny, mother's milk "curdled like a kind of cheese" when a nursing woman came into contact with sperm or became pregnant again.

This belief was common knowledge, and few questioned it. Some doctors also provided other rationale for the practice of using wet nurses. Roman doctor Soranus of Ephesus made allowances for women to use wet nurses so that "the mother can avoid aging prematurely from the daily energy that nursing consumes." Their real concern was that their women's breasts would not sag. Silicone was not on the horizon.

Wet nurses were usually hired as independent contractors for about two years. During this time, they were not permitted to engage in sexual relations and they could be fined if they became pregnant. Before a mother selected a wet nurse, she reportedly tasted her milk and felt her breasts. Rather like picking a ripe melon, she was looking for breasts that were full and firm, not hard or spongy.

Not everyone agreed with the practice of using a wet nurse. Plutarch, an ancient Greek moralist, had already condemned what he called, "this vile practice of hiring wet nurses and sacrificing tender victims to the greed and avarice of borrowed mothers."

But Pliny's myth had legs. The practice of using wet nurses continued to grow and by the Middle Ages every mother who could afford a wet nurse had one. Wet nurses became so common that books giving child care advice included instructions for how wet nurses should live and what they should eat or drink to increase the flow of their milk and make it healthy. The suggestions ranged from swallowing earthworms to eating the breasts of animals such as goats, which produce an ample supply of milk.

The belief that sperm spoiled milk and pregnancy poisoned it remained in place throughout the Middle Ages. The perpetuation of this myth continued to boost the popularity of wet nurses, despite the arguments of a growing number of doctors.

One physician, Laurent Joubert, said, "The woman I hold dearest in the world has nursed all my children, so full of milk is she, and I have not stopped sleeping with her for that reason, and I make love to her as a good husband should to his better half, following the dictates of marriage, and thank God, our children have been well nourished and are thriving. I give no advice to others that I do not myself follow. Unsatisfied desire is the major threat to milk." (Now, this guy was onto something!)

However, by the eighteenth century the popularity of hiring a wet nurse had grown so immense that nearly everyone who lived in a European city, no matter how rich or poor, contracted the services of a wet nurse. A police report written in Paris at the end of 1780 stated that less than 1,000 babies, out of the 21,000 born in Paris that year, were breast-fed by their own mothers. Another 1,000 were nursed by women who lived with the infant's family. But a shocking 19,000 were transported to wet nurses who lived in the suburbs, or further out into the countryside. It may seem amazing, but myths such as those of good old Pliny can last for eons.

We all have our personal myths that stay with us from childhood throughout our lives. Many cultures have strong opinions about pregnancy and sex. Many cultures are completely opposed to it as a matter of course. For instance, in some male-dominated traditions from Asia or the Middle East, it is believed that the woman must remain "pure" during the pregnancy, and it is acceptable for the man to have sex with another woman if he cannot endure the wait. Obviously, modern couples today must learn to evaluate their cultural traditions and decide which ones they want to adhere to when such views get in the way of their intimacy and long-term happiness.

How you feel about sex is often based on the messages you have been given throughout your upbringing. We learn from our parents and religious institutions. We learn from our peers and from our neighborhoods. We also learn from the climate of the times. If you are a student of popular culture, it is apparent that the young couples of the 1950s had a much different attitude about sex then the love children of the '60s. The 1970s ushered in all kinds of societal changes with the advent of such popular books as the groundbreaking *Joy of Sex*. A free spiritedness at that time gave couples permission to experiment and explore the possibilities for pleasure.

During the 1970s, an effort to create a normal and peaceful approach to sexuality began. Women were freed from the fear of pregnancy and were recognized as having needs that should be met as much as the needs of her lover.

During the 1980s certain diseases entered our language and curtailed some of the free spiritedness. The attitude of people toward sex returned to one of fear. This has become the myth that many couples carry into their marriages and ultimately into their sex life. Even though a monogamous love relationship joined together with pregnancy is not obviously subject to these fears, the subconscious does not easily forget the fear that has been the underlying factor in the development of one's sexuality. It may be safe and okay to say "yes" and to enjoy oneself, but is the fear ever going to fully go away unless it is confronted?

When a couple trusts one another and is preparing to have a baby together, this is a perfect time to overcome myths that pervade their sex life. Intimacy is something that is developed. By ridding yourself of the myths that follow you throughout your relationship, you will be able to enjoy sex during pregnancy and in the many years of bliss you can share together in the years to come.

Chapter Three

❧

Keeping the Fire Burning

Let's review. Sex is good. Sex is important for pregnant couples. Maintaining your love affair is the most important thing you can do for your relationship as you take on the new responsibilities of parenting. I am not suggesting that your new life as parents be self-focused to the detriment of your baby. As you grow as parents you will want to raise your child in a child-centered home. However, sometimes couples forget that they are lovers, and make their home *only* child centered. Aside from the damage this does to their relationship, it actually leads to the creation of a little monster who will probably rule a couple's life for the rest of their days. Contrary to current child-rearing methods, children do not need to be the center of every parent's universe.

We have a very confused outlook on child rearing because there is so much divorce. When you have children in two households at the same time they become the center of everyone's universe. Somehow this attitude has spilled over into the realm of the intact family. Perhaps it is because many couples wait until they are older and more successful to have children in the first place, or perhaps there are just so many more fun ways to indulge our children these days.

Having a child-centered house with balance means that the parents have a connected and important relationship with each other. This means that the child can't divide them when there are important decisions to make. This also means that there is a clear division between the parents' life and the life of the child. Many problems arise when children do not see their parents as authority figures.

If the parents are too "into each other" to the detriment of the child, other problems will arise. What I am suggesting is that you do not forget that you love each other not only as sex objects, but also as partners. When you share the stages of life with someone, you want to be secure that you are loved and desired.

There are definite things you can do to keep things hot. For example, ladies, don't frump out. Just because you are becoming a momma, don't get into the perpetual flannels. It is much more comfortable to live in your scruffies, but you don't want to forget that you are a woman underneath all of that maternity wear. It is wise to get into the habit now of maintaining your grooming rituals and your sense of pride in your appearance. You are going to be tired and stressed. When your baby is born you are going to be lucky if you get a shower.

You may not be at your sexiest now that you are growing a baby, but you want to have the attention to which you have become accustomed. Your husband will show his love in many ways, but if it is sexual attention you are after, you need to remember one of your greatest advantages. Men are visual. So when possible, try to remember this. He isn't going to focus on what your mind says is major girth. Many men find their pregnant wives to be an incredible turn on. You glow. Your breasts are full. How can he resist you?

But help it along. Both men and women become complacent about their appearances after they've been in a relationship for a while. They are either not aware of how much their partners want to be visually aroused or they don't care. These are the women who feel like they "have him," so they start walking around in sweats and baggy T-shirts, with no makeup and their hair flopped up in a ponytail. A lot of women say, "Hey, I should be able to be myself. He should love me for me."

To which I say, why lose an opportunity to maintain your sexual power? Visual stimulation has little to do with love—it is what is erotic. Touching is great, too, but sexiness is a good opener and starts things moving in the right direction.

To keep your relationship hot and spontaneous, it has to be nurtured. So, once in a while surprise him. When he comes home from work, instead of greeting him in your floppy ponytail and your baggy sweats, plan something special. About an hour before he's expected at home, slip into some sexy lingerie and then carry on with whatever you were planning to do. When he sees you sitting at the computer, cooking dinner, or reading, while acting like nothing's new, it will blow his mind. Trust me, he's going to grab you and want to ravish you.

Sexy lingerie you say? You would be surprised how much sexy lingerie is available for pregnant women. And it *is* sexy. A pregnant body is beautiful. There are nighties that accentuate whatever you would like. Take advantage of your cleavage. It is certainly one of the highlights of your pregnant shape.

You don't have time or energy for major grooming or lingerie surprises? Use the power of your mind. Think of how beautiful and sexy you are and you will become exactly what you believe yourself to be. There is nothing more beautiful and sexy than a woman who relishes her own femininity.

Men: don't frump out either. Although the comfort level of marriage and pregnancy can cause all of us to relax and let go, don't forget that part of desirability is image. Remember to wear cologne and to do whatever you do to stay sexy. Women are not necessarily as visual, but they definitely respond to attitude and the sense that you really care.

Now lets get to the nitty gritty. If you or your partner are having doubts about the ability to enjoy sex during your pregnancy, let me put your mind at ease. Contrary to some beliefs, the sex you have during pregnancy can be some of the best sex you'll ever have. A woman's sexual pleasure is magnified during pregnancy because all of her sex organs and genitalia are more sensitive. When a woman who isn't pregnant is aroused, the physical response of her body is for blood to rush to her genitals and the surrounding tissues. When she's pregnant, the blood is already there. It's almost like being in a nine-month state of pre-orgasmic pleasure.

Because of this, it's much easier to have an orgasm during pregnancy. Many women experience their first intravaginal orgasms during their pregnancy. Other women have multiple orgasms for the first time. So it can be a really wonderful time to find out what your body's actually capable of experiencing. For example, if a woman has been non-orgasmic or has had trouble achieving orgasm before pregnancy, her ability to achieve orgasm during pregnancy acts as a reassurance. Many women who have never climaxed before or have had a hard time think there's something wrong with them. "Well, maybe it's just my body. Maybe my body's not capable." And they find out that their bodies are very capable.

Not only that, but now that she knows she can orgasm, sex is a whole new ballgame. And so it will encourage her, after she has the baby, to go back and replicate the conditions that allowed her orgasms to happen. Usually, women simply need more or better foreplay so that their genitals and tissues are in a state that allows them to reach a climax. But now that she has tasted the heat of the flame, she is definitely going to want to keep things hot.

For the women who have been enjoying orgasms all along, pregnancy is a chance to get to know their bodies even better. Since all the sensations are magnified, you experience your body on a whole new level. Learning more about your preferences and how your body works will unlock countless realms of possibility. For instance, a lot of women don't know that their bodies are capable of producing orgasms from a number of different regions. If you touch those sensitive areas in different combinations, you can produce myriad sensations. Like any orgasmic woman knows, one orgasm can feel radically different from another. Some feel tingly, some feel squeezy, some make the bottoms of your feet hot, and so on. Basically, your body is an open book right now, for both you and your mate to read! Learn what you can and you'll be putting it to great use for many years to come.

What about the Men?

Most men I have asked say that sex during their partner's pregnancy is great, but different. The primary difference, aside from alternate sex positions, is the way a woman's vagina feels. It may feel softer, fuller, or not as snug as it felt before. The difference adds an element of variety to your lovemaking, and your partner may even prefer the "new you." Some men say that the lack of a tight fit is more than made up for by their partner's new level of excitement and enthusiasm. One of the biggest turn ons for a man is having sex with a woman who openly shows him how much she enjoys it.

Another difference can be the degree of moisture in the vagina. There are times when a pregnant woman will literally be changing panty liners a few times a day, and other times when no matter how much foreplay, her vagina may still feel dry. It's perfectly okay and advisable to use a lubricant as long as it doesn't have a spermicide and it's not petroleum based, like Vaseline. Olive oil is a good choice. It's very natural. It's clean and edible. Astroglide or K-Y lubricating jelly are good, too, but if you use them, think about the order in which you proceed because they don't taste very good.

"Making Love" Versus "Getting Off"

One of the problems that lots of couples run into, pregnant or not, is the division over wanting to "make love," versus wanting to "get off." More women than men complain about the focus on the goal. This is because many times women are simply left unsatisfied. Men who learn how much more pleasurable it is for them if they take their time to bring their women to the heights of pleasure never want to rush through the process again. A quickie is fine, but a lovemaking event is even better.

Men believe that women want wine and roses every time they make love. Even the women think this is what they want. What women really want is time to become aroused. This can begin with wine and roses, but it can be accomplished just as well with some strategic, gentle, and sexy caresses. Women will trade roses for fulfilling orgasms any day.

Making love begins with the feelings of the partners *outside* the bedroom. If you love each other outside the bedroom, you can simply enjoy "getting off" sometimes and be happy while at other times you can choose to luxuriate in each other. Making love is not determined by what happens in the bedroom. It's determined by the entire context of the relationship. You don't always need to take a long time to have satisfying sex. Taking your time helps because it sometimes takes more time for women to become aroused to the point of easy orgasm. When you become comfortable enough with each other, you can learn what it takes to make the experience more satisfying for both of you.

It would not surprise you, based on everything we have discussed so far, that many couples report that marital satisfaction goes down (sometimes significantly) after the birth of their first child. One of the primary reasons this happens is because the marriage and love affair, as they knew it, has ended. In my opinion they needlessly let it die. They do nothing to keep it alive. They are now Mommy and Daddy. While they may still love each other very much, they are allowing their new roles to undermine their connection as lovers. The only thing that you do with your lover that you don't do with anyone else is have sex. Make the commitment and the effort to keep your sex life hot and your role as lovers intact, and you will discover that being lovers and parents is a magnificent combination.

Continuing to be lovers doesn't mean that you have to have sex all the time. It means that you want to stay physically and sexually connected. Just lying naked next to each other and talking and touching and tickling and caressing goes a long way. If it leads to some fireworks, so be it.

What's Sexy? What's Not?

We live in a culture that surrounds us with messages about sex. From advertising to music to movies, we are bombarded every day with sexually explicit messages. Unfortunately, the men portrayed in these messages often have the chiseled, perfectly symmetrical proportions of Greek statues, and the women look like Barbie dolls who have mysteriously come to life. If we buy into the media concept that these looks define "sexy," we miss out on the innate sexiness that is unique to every one of us.

Up until recently, the media's take on a pregnant woman's body was as backward as some of our stories in Chapter Two. The media has portrayed pregnancy as anything but sexy. A pregnant woman might be portrayed as cute, funny, clumsy, pious, caring, or nurturing, but she rarely has even an ounce of sex appeal.

Fortunately, a number of celebrities have become proud parents and have paraded proudly with pizzazz. You can hardly turn the pages of a pop culture or gossip magazine without seeing the pregnant pulchritude. Pregnant women are beautiful and sexy and I am grateful to the celebrities who have been bold in their statements. Our perspectives are shifting to a true appreciation of the feminine pregnant form. Pregnant women are seen more as goddesses than something to be hidden until the birth.

Maternity fashion has changed. Not so many years ago most maternity wear consisted of poof sleeves and gingham. Though fine for some women, they are just not for everyone. Now, wonderful clothing lines cater specifically to pregnant women. There are dresses for work and casual outfits; I already told you about the sexy lingerie. I felt very sexy when I was pregnant—I was even comfortable with my maternity thong! (They are not for everyone, especially if you do not like thongs when you are not pregnant.) I loved having so many sexy things to choose from. You can enjoy some hot times with the right mood and outfits to go along with your plans. Don't worry if the lingerie is not the most comfortable. You probably will not be wearing it for very long. You will notice how nicely you fill out the bustline. Definitely make the "breast" of your womanliness.

Do not for one minute buy into the attitude that fatitude is bad. First of all pregnant women are not fat, they are pregnant with child. Second, most men I know love women with a little more meat on them. When you are pregnant the weight just congregates more to one area than to other places. It is important that women do not feel self-conscious about their expanded shape. So much of what one believes influences everything else. If a woman focuses on her girth as being something unsexy, she will have a very hard time feeling good about herself, and her sexual self-confidence will plummet. If a man tries to initiate sexual foreplay with a woman who believes she is as big as a cow or a beached whale, she will not be responsive. Men, it is to your advantage to help your woman feel as sexy and desirable as possible. It is not comfortable for a woman to carry a baby inside her for nine months. The least you can do is to make the woman you love feel like she is still a woman and not a receptacle.

Men: Your pregnant mate is the same woman she was before she expanded to what will become, to her, massive proportions. If you forget this you may hesitate to initiate sex. I will show you how to do it despite the changing shape of the sexual environment. If you choose to wait until the child is born you might find that your wait will be a lot longer than that. Be creative, be supportive, and view this time as your investment in your future. Your wife will not be pregnant forever. How you treat her during this time will be remembered. Women never forget things like this.

What Do Men Find Sexy?

The number one thing that men find sexy in a woman is self-confidence. If you take a fashion model type and put her next to a woman who has an attractive face and an average body, most men will be attracted to the one who is the most comfortable in her own skin. This is a very important point, because so often women sell themselves short simply because they don't look like the photographs they see on magazine covers.

Pregnant women are especially vulnerable to loss of sexual self-esteem. Women need to reassure themselves that they are beautiful, but husbands can certainly help. There are no valid stereotypes of what is sexy. So it may as well be you. You define what it is and you define what it is that you see in each other.

Beauty begins on the inside. Sexuality begins in the same place. That's why one of the most attractive and appealing traits a woman can have is a sense of her own self worth. Basically, she knows she's worthy of great things in life, including love, a great partner, and a happy family. So one of the things a pregnant woman can do to increase her sexiness is to believe that she is sexy. By dispelling the myths and opinions of those around her and concentrating on how she feels during this glorious period of womanhood, the pregnant woman can experience her greatest inner and outer glow.

The way a woman feels about herself is a far more pervasive factor in how men and others respond than how she compares with other people. I have spoken to thousands of men about this, and ninety-nine out of a hundred say that a woman who feels that she's sexy *is* sexy.

These same men also say they're attracted to a woman who enjoys life, knows how to laugh, loves a good meal, and has some meat on her bones. No matter what the media would have us believe, men would rather have a woman who takes good care of herself, who loves who she is, who loves life, and who's comfortable in her own skin. Men find that incredibly appealing.

Women: Rejoice in your femininity, rejoice in being a woman, and feel sexy. Learn how to enjoy life. Learn to be comfortable with yourself, and realize that people will believe what you project. If you walk into a room and you project, "I like myself the way I am. I am sexy. I am lovable. I'm adorable. I'm intelligent and you want to get to know me," they will have no choice but to agree. Who can resist that?

But, beware of the opposite. If you walk into a room projecting, "I'm not okay because I need to lose weight and I don't measure up," that's what people are going to believe. Although men are visual and enjoy a woman's physical attributes, they are far less critical of a woman's appearance than a woman is of her own. People, and men in particular, feel beauty as much as they see it. The bottom line is that if you feel sexy and are enjoying life as you proceed through your pregnancy, your partner will reflect this belief as well.

Seeing Is Believing

As I have already said, we know that men are very visual creatures. It's as if their eyes have a direct line to their penises. I don't care how intellectual, sensitive, liberal, or objective your mate may be, he notices how you look, and he gets turned on when you look sexy. This may sound like a contradiction of what I just said, but it's not. Though it's true that men find self-confidence, sexual self-esteem, and zest for life very attractive and appealing, it's also true that they are often most easily aroused by a visual image. So don't feel shy when you are wearing your sexy maternity lingerie. Try putting on a little modeling show for your mate and see what happens. You'll be amazed at how sexy it makes you feel when you behave seductively in your maternity lingerie. Your mate's response will be memorable and a boost to your self-image as well.

You are thinking of this because you are pregnant, but don't forget the sexy dance after the baby is born. You will want to steal time away from the little one for some one-on-one. This is a great activity to plan for one of those romantic interludes. Lust and passion can be transporting.

Don't worry if you are not up to doing this all the time. You do live in the real world. I spent a lot of my pregnancy sleeping. But when you are feeling energetic, take the time out. Strut your stuff whenever you can. Tell your husband to do a little strutting as well. Play a little grab-the-ass whenever you can. Men love being treated as sex objects. As the reality of impending fatherhood hits them, they can also have their doubts about their continued desirability.

Overcoming the Barriers

There are numerous hurdles for couples to jump if they want to remain lovers as they become parents. Many of these hurdles are created by the physical and emotional changes and conditions that a woman experiences during the pregnancy. These "sex stoppers," such as morning sickness, backache, and tender breasts, are discussed in Chapters Four, Five, and Six according to which trimester they will most likely arise. As troublesome as these challenges can be, they are, at least, obvious.

The hurdles that tend to be the highest and hardest to jump are the ones you don't automatically notice. As you have already learned, these are the deeper-seeded ideas, beliefs, hang-ups, and miscellaneous mental programs that set off alarms and trigger behavior that is anything but desirable in both you and your spouse. Over the course of your pregnancy it will be wise to take a pulse on your relationship from time to time. If one or both of you are behaving in a way that is damaging to your intimate connection, it is imperative that you deal with it pronto! Don't put it off until the baby is born, because there's a good chance that if you ignore it, it will get worse. On the other hand, if you face it and work through it, you take the fulfillment level of your relationship up another notch.

A Note to the Men

There will be times during the pregnancy when your partner will simply not want to have sex. Although lovemaking is a valuable and important aspect of pregnancy, I'm not going to tell you that if you do A, B, and C, you'll get D, because the fact is you may not get D. And when you don't get the sex or the attention you want, you're going to have to focus on other things to give you that sense of fulfillment in bonding and love that sex normally brings about. (More about this in Chapter Seven.)

The Lost Sex Toy

For couples who had great sex before pregnancy, there is often a sense that each partner is a sexual plaything—ready, willing, and available at any time for a morning romp, an afternoon quickie, or a slow massage ending in multiple orgasms. For many couples, though, the sexual spontaneity disappears during pregnancy and especially after the baby is born, causing mates to feel less intimate and more distant from each other. Men, in particular, often have a sense of loss, or a feeling that they have been "replaced" by the baby. Couples should remain aware of this and maintain open and honest communication about their sexual needs and desires.

Out to Pasture

Men often experience a sense of being sent "out to pasture" after the baby is conceived, noticing that their mate gives all her attention to the pregnancy. The man may react to this by feeling like he is no longer wanted or needed, now that his "job" is done. He may become resentful and distant, sometimes even toward the baby (the proverbial distant father).

If your partner was a raging horn dog before you got pregnant, and now he's acting like sex isn't important—or worse, seems to be repelled by the idea—it generally means one of two things: he's either uncomfortable with your changing shape or he believes one of the many myths about having sex during pregnancy.

If he has a case of "myth-information," having him read about his concerns in Chapters One and Two of this book should help to put his mind at ease and help him to expand his perceptions. It would also be a good idea to have your doctor address your mate's concerns at your next visit.

If your partner is put off by your changing shape, he may or may not be able to admit it, and even if he does share this with you, chances are he won't be able to tell you "why" he feels the way he does. Most of the time these feelings have a lot to do with what culture he grew up in—his family's views, his church's views, and/or society's views of the pregnant female body and how it "should be" treated.

One way that you'll know something is going on for your partner is if he becomes evasive. You may notice that he's not talking sexy like he used to. It's not that he's not loving, but he may not be as engaging in sex talk. If he's already been reassured that there's no medical reason why you can't continue your sex life, then you know that it's probably in issue of culture or upbringing.

As much as you may want to run from this, you have to confront it. Ask him point-blank, "What is it that you don't like about having sex while I'm pregnant?" If you want an honest answer, you're going to have to refrain from feeling hurt or angry when you ask, and especially when you listen to his answers. Remind yourself that he is not rejecting "you." He is rejecting some stereotypical belief or idea that he probably has never examined or questioned before.

Be objective and help him to get to the bottom of his discomfort. When you do, you're going to find out that it's nothing personal. It's most likely that his views have been warped by the media and popular culture. If a man can say, "Well, gee, I hate it because you're fatter than you used to be and it's not so sexy," he just opened the door to the next question.

"Well, why isn't it sexy?"

Eventually he's going to get down to his own true feelings and will realize that his perceptions have been shaped by what other people think, what he's read or seen on television. So, just ask the questions. It's going to require you to be very strong, because even though it's not personal, it feels personal.

You can work through your feelings if you talk about them. Being pregnant is as sexy as a woman can be. Bringing a baby into the world is the most powerful thing a woman can do. A woman needs to realize that her ability to give life is the ultimate in power and it is very sexy.

Maintaining Your "Sex Pot" Image

Day by day, week by week, the sex pot that you used to be seems to be mysteriously slipping away. Contrary to what you may think, this doesn't happen because you're getting bigger and closer to giving birth. It happens because you begin to disassociate from your role as "sexy" and associate with your role as a mother. As we discuss throughout this book, it is not necessary to give up being sexy in order to be a good mother. Please believe me! We are capable of playing many different roles in our lives and embracing all of them. We can be sexy and still be a good writer, or a good cook, or a good tennis player. Why, then, is the concept of being sexy and being a good mother still so foreign to our society's way of thinking?

Women need to somehow maintain their image as a sex pot in their partner's eyes. This means they may need to be more sexually aggressive than they're used to being. If your partner was initiating sex 75 percent of the time, you may have to take the lead for a while. I know it's difficult, because sometimes when you're pregnant the last thing you feel like doing is having sex. Even so, I highly recommend initiating sex and doing other things that clearly say, "I am still your sex pot. I still desire you. You turn me on." Really focus on being his lover.

A woman who immerses herself in the role of "expectant mother," and forsakes her "inner sex goddess," is running a high risk of creating a rift in the relationship. When a woman does this, her partner is most likely going to feel deeply rejected and possibly like less of a man. It is these types of feelings that pave the way for a man to have an affair.

Initiating sex is the key. It will not only keep your bond of intimacy strong, but if you're not feeling turned on, it will awaken your own desires. Let him know how sexy it makes you feel to be pregnant, how your changing body is so "ready to love," because you feel so powerful and feminine.

You can also help him to ease some of his fears by using a clever combination of actions and words. I highly recommend connecting your new role of motherhood with sexuality. Take his hand and lightly rub it around on your belly while telling him how sexy and powerful you feel. Then take his other hand and put it on your breast and kiss him. You're connecting your belly (motherhood) with your breasts (sexual pleasure and motherhood). Now, move his hand down so that one hand is on your belly and one hand is on your vagina. So subconsciously it's going to signal to him, without him even knowing it, that your body is still Pleasure Party Central.

Not only that, but you're giving him permission to enjoy your body and you're telling him that you're still sexy and desirable and you still want him. It doesn't necessarily have to lead to intercourse. What we're doing here is subtly ingraining in the back of his mind that "I'm still your lover and I desire you." Pleasuring him with your hands, your mouth, or anything that will keep you in the role of lover as opposed to mother is very important. Because when the baby comes, he is going to see you as a mother and if you don't already have your role as "lover" firmed up in his mind, it could be a difficult transition.

Getting What You Need

Telling your mate what you want can be simple and effective if you approach each other in a way that doesn't set off defenses.

Needs and desires should be expressed in terms of, "I want," or "I need," instead of "You do this," or "You don't do that." Blaming, nagging, whining, or making demands is not going to work and you're going to push your partner further away with any or all of these tactics. The best way to avoid all of this is to be direct. And this goes double for the women.

Men cannot stand it when women hint or make suggestions. When you need something, go directly to your partner and say, "Listen. I'm feeling a little insecure right now. I know this is new for you. It's new for me, too. Here's what I need. Can you give this to me? I need you to tell me that I'm beautiful. I need you to tell me that I look sexy."

Men love that, because they dislike having to second-guess women. They find us incredibly hard to figure out and very unpredictable, and they love it when we give them the answer to the question. So go in there and tell them what you need, because it takes the guesswork out of it.

Men are incredibly fearful of letting women down. High up on most men's priority list of values is appearing manly, strong, and capable in front of their mates. You do your partner a big favor by taking the guesswork out of it and telling him what you need, because then it allows him to fulfill one of his highest values as a man, namely taking care of you and seeing to it that your needs are met. Go in there and tell him what you need, because that's what he wants.

Definitely don't whine, nag, complain, or use guilt. I call these "guerrilla tactics." A common guerrilla tactic is for a woman to try to get what she wants by setting herself up for failure. Instead of saying, "Listen, I'm feeling a little insecure about my body. My body is changing. Could you please tell me that I look sexy and beautiful," she'll sabotage what she needs by playing a no-win type of game. She might be reading a fashion magazine and she'll show a gorgeous sexy model to her mate and say, "You wish I looked like that, don't you?" Or she'll walk into the room and say, "Oh, I don't look too good today," or "Oh, I'm getting fat." She's trying to provoke something positive, but she's actually provoking something negative. You know the old joke about, "Honey, does this make me look fat?" There's no winning answer to that question.

There's one more important side note here. While being direct is the rule, be thoughtful about when and where you're doing it. Private issues should never be discussed with anyone else present unless you're in a therapy session together. And don't discuss problems in the bedroom. Do it in the living room, do it outside at a café where you have some privacy, anywhere but the bedroom. The bedroom is not the place to talk about problems—especially if those problems involve your sex life. The only talk about sex that should happen in the bedroom is the sort that leads to a more satisfying sensation, such as, "How is this feeling for you? How can I make this more enjoyable for you?"

In those moments when you're doubting your sex appeal, remember this:

> *You are the most sexy when you're pregnant,*
> *because it's the ultimate display of power as a human being.*
>
> *Only women have this power.*
> *A woman who's comfortable in her own pregnant body,*
> *and who isn't afraid to show it,*
> *is the most powerful human being on the face of the earth.*

Chapter Four shows how to bypass the sex stoppers that are most common during the first trimester of pregnancy.

Chapter Four

First Trimester: Feeling Sexy Despite Feeling Sick

If you're like most pregnant women, you're tired, your breasts are tender to the touch, and nausea is becoming a way of life. So, it's no surprise that your desire for lovemaking can plummet during the first trimester of pregnancy.

But don't despair! While there may actually be moments when the very thought of sex makes you retch, you can still take advantage of the times when you're feeling good. Keeping your sexual intimacy and passion in place during this physical and hormonal roller coaster ride takes some effort and a flexible balance of planning and spontaneity, but the rewards are plentiful. As I promised in the first chapter, you will discover that making love during this special time creates a more intimate bond with your partner, deepens the level of trust and honesty in your marriage, and helps you to feel happier and healthier throughout the pregnancy, and afterward.

Sensual lovemaking and hot, steamy sex play are among the most important ways to stay connected with your partner whether you're pregnant or not. But sharing sex during pregnancy is even more important because many men feel left out and isolated during this time. Though we women tend to feel most connected to our mates when we're talking and hugging, most men feel emotionally closest to us during or after sex. That's why so many men who are normally quiet and reserved about what's going on in their lives are willing to open up and talk after an intimate encounter. If you want to know the depth of your husband's heart about a topic, get him to talk about it after he's had an orgasm and before he falls asleep. By the way, that's another reason to have more sex in the morning and afternoon. By the time you're both in bed for the night, there will rarely be much energy left for lovemaking, and if there is, he'll probably yearn to roll over and go fast asleep right afterward. Making love in the afternoon, and lounging in bed or on the sofa together for a few hours, just touching, sharing, and laughing is a wonderful way to heighten your marriage's intimacy level and deepen the trust that you have for each other.

As far as the actual lovemaking goes, during the first trimester, you can keep doing whatever you've been doing, with just a few exceptions. The first exception is if you are in a high-risk pregnancy and your doctor tells you not to have intercourse, not to orgasm, or both. (More about this in Chapter Seven.)

The second exception concerns sex toys. If you've been using dildos or other objects that are inserted into the vagina, I suggest that you pack them safely away for now. Fortunately, you don't have to put away your vibrator, you just need to keep it outside your vagina. Inserting dildos or vibrators into your vagina during pregnancy increases your risk of infections, and if they're "supersized," they can damage your tender vaginal tissues. If you enjoy playing with "butt plugs," you can still use them on your husband, but I don't recommend inserting anything into your rectum during pregnancy. These tissues are tender too, and infection is a potential problem in this area as well. You can bring all your toys back out, and even buy some new ones, after you've recovered from the birth of your baby. For now, explore other ways to tease and please each other.

The third category of exceptions, and the one that affects couples the most, are the physical and hormonal changes. New physical sensations can make a pregnant woman feel out of sorts as her body adjusts to all those rapid changes. Meanwhile "pregnancy hormones" begin to run the show. There *are* women who somehow manage to sail through the first trimester, boasting of no headaches, nausea, or fatigue, but they are few and far between.

Bypassing the First Trimester's
Top Ten Sex Stoppers

Plenty of potential sex stoppers can pull the plug on your passion during pregnancy. However, thanks to experience, increased understanding, and modern science, you can outsmart and outmaneuver even some of the peskiest problems!

1. Misguided Myths: Sex Can Hurt the Baby

We covered this myth in Chapter One and showed how it got started in Chapter Two. But in case you missed it, rest assured that having sex will not endanger the baby in any way, shape, or form. Unless you're in a high-risk pregnancy, you can proceed without fear. By the end of the first trimester, the baby is still only a few inches long and is very safe within the womb. If your husband thinks he's an exception to this rule because he prides himself in his "larger than average" size, tell him not to take the flattery too far. Even a foot-long fantasy won't reach the fetus.

Meanwhile, although sex, in itself, can't hurt the baby, "dirty sex," can do damage to the mother and the baby! A pregnant woman is far more prone to certain types of vaginal infections, so cleanliness is a must. Showering together before sex is a great way to begin foreplay and it ensures that your bodies and hands are germ-free. I suggest lathering each other up with a natural shower gel, then getting into the slippery sensation that your skin creates when you rub against each other. Make sure you have a non-slip bath mat or the equivalent in your tub so that you keep your footing! After you're both squeaky clean, gently towel off each other, taking time to caress the areas around the genitals. Depending on how you're both feeling, this can be an urgent, "I have to have you," quickie, or can unfold over the course of an entire evening or afternoon.

2. Twenty-Four-Hour-a-Day Morning Mayhem

A pregnant woman's physical experiences can range from bouts of mild queasiness to what I call "twenty-four-hour-a-day morning mayhem." Even if you could choose when to feel sick each day, morning sickness would still be a miserable thing. But the reality of the situation—which is that you can feel suddenly and violently ill with no notice and at the most inconvenient times—just adds to the frustration. In retrospect, running out of a staff meeting with your hand clasped over your mouth may seem funny, but there's nothing even remotely amusing about it when it's happening. Women who have never been pregnant have a hard time understanding the concept of making food choices based on what will taste okay "in reverse," but those of you who have been through this before will know exactly what I'm talking about.

The good news is that your body is reacting this way because it's making the physiological and hormonal changes to create a safe and nurturing haven for your developing baby. Believe it or not, nausea is a sign that your baby is healthy and that your body is doing what it's supposed to do. The bad news, aside from the obvious, is that it's hard to feel sexy when you're vomiting, or about to.

As any woman who has been pregnant will tell you, morning sickness can happen at *any* time of day as your hormonal system goes crazy. Of course, this is one of the first challenges that can put a damper on sexual intimacy. You may find it encouraging to know that morning sickness usually subsides or ends abruptly in the second trimester, so hold on. Meanwhile, stock up on soda crackers, chewing gum, and other tummy-calming munchies. Stash them all over your house, in your handbags, and in your car. During the first few months I was pregnant, I couldn't leave home without my soda crackers!

You can also add some safe herbal teas to your pantry. For example, chamomile tea is very soothing and it won't hurt the baby. It's also great at settling your stomach and relieving stress. Mint tea assists digestion and combats gas and bloating. Many people also find the aroma of mint teas stimulating and energizing. Another herb that some women swear by for nausea and motion sickness is gingerroot. You can use it in cooking, make a tea with it, or buy it in capsules. Some women say that drinking ginger ale offers similar results, but there's nothing like the real thing! (**Caution:** Herbs and herbal teas that should be avoided during pregnancy include cohosh, comfrey, goldenseal, and raspberry.) You can also add fresh lemon juice to water or carbonated mineral water to ease nausea and help your digestion.

Nausea is a part of pregnancy. It's hormonal and it's probably going to be with you for at least a couple of months. That's why it's important—

for both you and your husband—to capitalize on the times when you're feeling good. For women who feel queasy in the morning or evening, now's the time to try an afternoon delight! The trick is to let your partner know when you're feeling good, either by telling him, or better yet, by showing him.

Explain how you're feeling to your mate and ask him to bear with you. Let him know that you can make up for lost time during the second trimester, when your hormones will tend to make you very horny.

3. Hormonal Hurricanes

As your body prepares to create a new and unique human being, you experience numerous physical changes and tremendous hormonal shifts. One moment you're calm and joyful, and a few seconds later you burst into tears or lash out in anger at whatever (or whoever!) is in your path. Unfortunately, many men take their pregnant wife's emotional inconsistency and unpredictability personally. They can often feel like they are being unfairly attacked, blamed, or put down.

It's true that your hormones can play havoc with your emotions; sometimes you truly can't help how you feel. However, you *can* help how you act. Women who use the hormonal roller coaster to express pent up frustrations about their partner are asking for trouble. If you have something to deal with in your relationship, deal with it. But don't hide behind your hormones or use them to excuse your inconsiderate behavior. If you do, your husband's empathy for your condition will rapidly diminish.

The best way for couples to weather these storms is to be open and honest about what's going on, be patient, and stay intimately connected. The times when you're feeling good are the times to let your hubby know that you find him sexier than ever. Help him to understand what you're going through and ask him to share what he's experiencing. Most important, assure him that you love him and need him and tell him how grateful you are to be having a child with him.

4. Tired of Being Tired

Nearly every organ in your body is working overtime to prepare for your new baby; plus, you're developing new organs. A placenta is growing in your uterus to provide nourishment for your baby and the formation and growth of your baby's organs. Add to that the hormonal and physiological changes that you're experiencing, and it's no wonder you're tired.

For your sake, as well as your baby's, listen to the messages your body is giving you and nap as frequently as you can. Fatigue is Mother Nature's way of getting you to conserve your energy so that it can be used to create a new life. When you absolutely can't nap, at least take a few moments to de-stress and reenergize by closing your eyes, putting your feet up, and breathing deeply. Also, make sure your bedroom is cozy and as dark as possible so that you can get a good night's sleep.

Some women say that making love before going to bed helps them to sleep more deeply, so it's certainly worth trying! Meanwhile, when your partner is revved up and ready to go, and you can't stop yawning, try meeting each other halfway. You can help him reach orgasm with a "hand job" or participate by caressing him while he masturbates himself. You may discover that you're suddenly wide awake after all! But if not, that's okay. And it's also okay to say "no" when you simply don't have the energy. Consider stashing a few erotic magazines or videos that you can surprise your partner with during those times when your participation is absolutely not an option. This is a win-win way to compromise. Helping your husband to help himself is one of the nicest ways to say "no."

5. Your Bladder Becomes Your Boss

Frequent urination is common during the first few months of pregnancy and is caused by the pregnancy hormones that your body is producing. Later in the pregnancy the frequent urge to urinate occurs because your uterus presses on your bladder. But during the first trimester, your frequent trips to the bathroom are being triggered entirely by the new combination of hormones that your body is creating.

Don't let the inconvenience of frequent bathroom visits stop you from drinking plenty of water. Try to drink at least 64 ounces of pure, fresh water every day. Drink most of the water before dinnertime and you can reduce the frequency of getting up to urinate during the night. If you normally sleep on the side of the bed that is farthest away from the bathroom, you may want to switch sides with your husband. Though walking an extra fifteen feet doesn't make much difference for an occasional midnight pee, it quickly adds up when you're getting up several times a night.

Believe it or not, some women say the subtle feeling of needing to urinate actually turns them on, and they use this to their advantage. When I explained this to a group of pregnant women, one of them said she didn't want to have sex because "stopping the action for a pee break" killed the mood. I say, if you have to go, you have to go. Don't think of it as interrupting the mood. Think of it as practice for the near future. When your little one is born, there will be plenty of times when you will be interrupted during lovemaking. Now's the time to learn how to take a break, and then get right back into it. Once you've done it a few times, you'll see that it's really pretty easy. Some couples say that holding the mental picture of what their partner was doing before the time-out helps them to stay in the moment. Both men and women who practice this technique say that when they resume lovemaking, they are often just as aroused as they were when they left—sometimes more so.

6. Gagging: No Laughing Matter

Your taste buds and sense of smell can do a total about-face when you're pregnant. Tastes and aromas like fresh ground coffee or spicy foods, which you used to love, can become nausea triggers. Unfortunately, this phenomenon doesn't stop outside the bedroom door. For example, women who previously enjoyed the scent and taste of giving their partner oral sex may discover that it now sets off a gag reflex.

Some women hesitate to share this information with their husbands, because they don't want to hurt their feelings. However, by being honest about it, you open the door to finding pleasing solutions. You might also find out that he's experiencing something similar when he performs cunnilingus on you. Lots of men say that the scent and taste of a woman changes when she is pregnant. Some of these men like the differences; some do not.

Be patient with yourself and each other. Do your best to work around these triggers, or avoid them altogether when you know you're not up for it. Some couples sing the praises of edible chocolate body paints and taste pleasers like whipped cream. Some yummy-tasting body oils can be just enough to turn "not so sure about this" into "hey, this is pretty good," or at least, "this isn't bad!" Find out what works for you—*bon appétit!*

7. When Food Rules Your Life

Thanks to the hormonal merry-go-round that a pregnant woman is riding, she is likely to be plagued by food cravings. (Remember the frustrated pregnant woman in Chapter Two who couldn't satisfy her craving for a third bite of the baker?) Researchers are at odds about what causes some of the cravings that pregnant women have, but we do know that some cravings are triggered by the body's need for certain vitamins or minerals. For example, women often crave pickles, because the salt encourages the body to want more water, and more water is often what a pregnant woman needs the most! Even so, the joke about the mother-to-be who needs her husband to go out for pickles and ice cream at three o-clock in the morning isn't funny when you're that woman—or her husband!

The good news is that there's really nothing wrong with indulging your urges as long as you do it with moderation and common sense. One or two cookies, not the whole box. Remember that your baby is eating whatever you are eating, so satisfy your cravings as much as you can with healthy choices.

Foods to Avoid

fried and greasy foods	cabbage, cauliflower, and
high-fat foods	sauerkraut
foods with monosodium glutamate	caffeine
(MSG)	artificial sweeteners
spicy foods	

Healthy Comfort Foods—From Fruit to Nuts

applesauce	celery sticks
avocados	grapes
bananas	melons
berries	pears
carrot sticks	

eggplant	tomatoes
potatoes, white and sweet	yams
squash	zucchini
bagels	whole grain cereals
rice cakes	pasta
oatmeal	egg noodles
sherbet	yogurt
sorbet	
almonds	sunflower seeds
brazil nuts	soynuts
pumpkin seeds (nonsalted)	

8. Don't Touch Me There!

Your breasts may be tender and feel fuller. The areolas are beginning to darken in color from light pink to a deeper red. Your nipples may feel tingly, sore, warm, or extrasensitive. Your breasts might also throb and some women experience occasional shooting pains that can last for a few minutes, off and on. These sensations are caused by the increased blood flow to your breasts and the growth of milk glands.

The tenderness tends to subside after the first three months, but until it does, even the fabric of your bra against your nipples can alternate between being arousing and feeling like sand paper. If your husband is aroused by bringing your nipples to life with his mouth and tongue, he may have a hard time giving this up. It will be important for you to share with him just how incredibly tender you are right now.

Show him how to gently stroke and fondle you while barely touching your nipples, or avoiding them altogether if you prefer. Most women know that the nipple is not always the most exciting part of the breast to be touched. The lower curve of each breast is very, very sensitive (especially during pregnancy) and it's not painful to be touched. Try a spiraling method in which you take the fingertips and work from the outside of the breast in, avoiding the nipple.

As your breasts start to grow and become heavier, you may be surprised how much pressure your bra straps put on your shoulders and your back. A mutually beneficial way for your husband to stay connected with your breasts, without stimulating them, is to gently hold them up with his hands, taking the new weight off you for a moment. Have your hubby stand behind you and lift up each of your breasts in one of his hands. If you're wearing a bra at the time, it will send a wonderful wave of relief through your back and shoulders. If you're bare breasted, it will give you a respite from the heavy, pendulous feeling that pregnant breasts often acquire. For obvious reasons, this little exercise is appreciated more and more as the pregnancy progresses and your breasts continue to increase in cup size.

9. Unfounded Fears about Spotting

For a few months after becoming pregnant, some women experience light bleeding during the time they would normally be menstruating. You may also notice a little spotting after sexual intercourse. Many people are convinced that this is a warning sign meaning that sex is too much for the baby. If you or your husband believe this, it will certainly make you hesitant and uncomfortable about having intercourse. That's why it's so important to understand the facts about pregnancy and what's really going on in your body and with the developing fetus. The truth is that a little spotting after intercourse is rarely something to worry about. It generally happens because the vaginal tissues are more sensitive at this time. However, if there are more than a few spots, or if it continues for more than a day or two, you should consult your doctor.

10. OUCH!

Not very many women make it through the first trimester without some aches and pains. Some women feel discomfort or cramping in the lower abdomen and pelvis. You may also have mild pains on *both sides* of your waist when you stand up, sit down, or change positions. You are literally feeling your uterus growing and the sensations caused by the ligaments around your pelvis stretching. (If you have sharp pains, or pain on *only one side* of your pelvis, it could be a symptom of a more serious condition and should be reported to your doctor right away.)

The majority of the aches and pains are nothing to worry about, but that doesn't mean they don't hurt! Even if they just hurt a little, pain has a convincing way of stomping on your libido and will definitely cramp your style. I can't think of a single time when I was in pain, and then suddenly had the urge to have sex! My best advice is to "make hay when the sun shines," meaning take advantage of those days—or hours—when you feel better than usual.

Meanwhile, a great way to help yourself through the feelings of discomfort is to practice some gentle stretching and relaxation techniques. Just taking the time to lie on the floor and release the tension in your spine can feel incredible, but I recommend that you work toward gently increasing your flexibility for thirty minutes or more every day. Consider enrolling in a yoga class, or try a "stretching class" offered by your local Y.W.C.A. or a nearby athletic club. By increasing your flexibility and becoming more limber, you will have better circulation, improved aerobic ability, better muscle control, and less stress. You will feel much better and you'll be getting into better shape for giving birth.

This is also a wonderful time for your husband to demonstrate how much he loves and supports you by giving you a full-body, head-to-toe massage, complete with hot oil, music, and candlelight. Don't push the envelope too hard with this one. Although it's awesome to have the "total spa treatment" every now and again, I suggest you also take advantage of the mini–back rub while you're standing at the kitchen sink and the one-handed shoulder massage while he's watching the game and holding the remote or a beer in the other hand. Of course you deserve to have the best as often as possible, but be grateful for the small things, too—especially if he's coming through for you in a big way at other times.

One more word to the wise. An unbelievable number of men and women don't massage their mates because they either don't know how to do it, or they don't see the benefit of giving and receiving pleasure in this form. I could go on and on about this, but the bottom line is "Get over it." Plenty of books and videos teach basic massage techniques, and there are some very simple strokes and hand movements that everyone can learn. Just taking thirty minutes to look through a basic massage book or watch a video will be enough to get you started. With a little practice, you'll soon be making each other feel very good! Learning how to give a good massage gives you the skills to take each other to new heights of pleasure, with our without sex! Most women would agree that being married to a good masseur is just as important as being married to a good lover.

CHART 4.1   WHAT'S GOING ON INSIDE?

First Trimester Time Line

MONTH ONE

- Egg and sperm unite and fertilization occurs.
- The fertilized egg implants into the lining of the uterus.
- Hormones surge and the placenta and your baby begin to grow.
- Your baby grows to about the size of a grain of rice and begins to take shape.

MONTH TWO

- At the beginning of the second month, your baby is about the size of a pea and his or her heart is already divided into right and left chambers.
- Your baby has a fluttering heartbeat of 140 to 150 beats per minute. About one hundred thousand nerve cells are being created every minute.
- All the internal organs have formed and will continue to develop and grow throughout the pregnancy.
- By the end of the second month, your baby is about 1 inch long and is capable of beginning to move its body and limbs.

MONTH THREE

- The embryo is transforming into a fetus, which looks like a miniature human being.
- Your baby's teeth, fingernails, and toenails begin to form and so do the tongue and vocal cords.
- Your baby's external genitalia differentiate into male and female. By the end of this month, ultrasound pictures can often show whether your baby is a boy or a girl.
- Your baby can open and close its mouth, swallow amniotic fluid, and even hiccup. Your little miracle can also move its limbs, and open and close its fists.
- By the end of the first trimester, the baby is about 2½ to 3 inches long and weighs between a half of an ounce to an ounce.

Tips and Techniques for the
First Trimester

For many couples, the first few months of pregnancy can be a very sexy and magical time. But for those who aren't mentally and emotionally ready for the changes that pregnancy brings, the first trimester can be a living hell. Fortunately, the very thing that got you into this situation—namely sex—can once again turn the tide in your favor. Couples who make the commitment to stay sexually connected during pregnancy experience less stress, better health, and a more intimate connection.

Not only that, but once you both start feeling more relaxed about the physical and emotional changes that are occurring, you will probably agree that creating a child together adds a special element to a marriage, and often leads to more erotic and creative lovemaking.

Okay. So let's get going. First of all, for most women, feeling sexy is a state of mind. This is a great time to list all the things that you can do or think about that make you feel confident and erotic. Your list might include wearing high heels, working out, getting a facial or makeover, or focusing on a favorite fantasy. Every woman can tune into her own sex appeal and turn up the volume. If you've never embraced your inner sex goddess, now's the time. Really get in touch with whatever helps you to awaken the innate sexiness that you already possess, but may not be expressing yet.

It's certainly possible to attain this sexy state of mind by yourself, but it's much more fun when your husband is an active participant. That means if he doesn't already know what makes you feel sexy, it's high time you told him. If you've never been straightforward about this before, please don't kid yourself by thinking that he already knows—or worse yet, unrealistically believing that he "should know without you telling him." The reality is that if you want your partner to know what really makes you feel sexy, you have to be willing to tell him.

Once he knows what makes you feel irresistible, he can do his part to help. If, for example, you feel really sexy when you're wearing your stiletto heels, he can offer them to you with a wink and a smile. If he wants to be a real player, he'll step up to the plate with a handful of charming and seductive compliments—letting you know how desirable you are. When I was pregnant, my partner used to kiss the back of my neck and tell me how sexy he thought it was that I was carrying our baby. That was a big turn-on for me and was often the turning point between cuddling and making love.

Although you may not have the energy for really raucous, swinging-from-the-chandelier sex, by being proactive, you can still enjoy the heights and depths of your passion. In fact, many women say the best sex they've ever had was during pregnancy. The changes occurring in your body can make you more easily aroused and lead to more pleasurable orgasms. Another perk, which may surprise you, is that many men consider their pregnant partner "sexier than ever"!

During the first trimester, you still have all the freedom in the world to carry on sexually as you have been up until now. Unless you're in a high-risk pregnancy, any lovemaking positions that feel good are A-okay. I especially suggest positions that don't require a lot of physical effort on the pregnant woman's part.

Some low-effort positions for women include sitting in a chair or on the edge of the bed while your partner kneels or stands, and lying on your stomach or back, so you don't have to support yourself or move your body around a lot.

Keep in mind that with all of the hormonal and physical changes occurring in a pregnant woman's body, her sexual pilot light may need to be gently kindled to get it to really ignite. I suggest fanning this flame with attention, affection, and the right touch!

Science has proven that being touched and stroked strengthens our immune systems and decreases our levels of stress, anger, and anxiety. Stroking and touching each other is worth doing, just for the fun of it, but knowing that you are actually healing each other and your developing baby adds a new dimension to this intimate connection. Sensual touching is wonderful, in and of itself, and it can also be one of the best ways to prepare your mind and body for incredibly hot lovemaking.

For Him

First of all, there's nothing more arousing for a woman than a man who truly understands and *tells* her that he understands. "What can I do for you?" "How are you feeling?" "You sure look sexy." "You are so beautiful."

These types of questions and compliments are wonderfully affirming and have all the powers of a potent aphrodisiac! If you're not in the habit of voicing your concern and attraction for your wife, it's time to get in the habit, especially if you're committed to keeping your sex life strong throughout this pregnancy. I'm not going to tell you that there's a magic formula to getting your pregnant partner to want sex, because there isn't. But the more you support and understand her, and the less you whine and complain about your "needs," the more sex you're likely to have.

If there was ever a time to explore the erotic zones of the body that are outside of the genitalia, this is the time to do it! By avoiding touching your partner's genitals, and focusing on and touching areas like her arms, legs, neck, and so on, you ultimately create a sensation of arousal all over her body, from head to toe. Within minutes, these pleasurable body sensations will be felt throughout her body and she may suddenly find herself "in the mood."

You may not think of the tummy as an erogenous zone, but stroking and kissing the soft skin of the belly can send waves of delightful sensations rippling through your lover's body.

Kiss her all over her tummy and tell her how sexy it is that this area is where your baby is growing. Help her to lie down on her back, and put her legs together. While you kiss her stomach, tickle the fronts and insides of her legs with your fingertips. Gently tickle down to her ankles and back up her legs, stopping just below her genitals.

The sensation of feeling your touch right above and below her most sensitive zone will probably make her start to wriggle around and there's a good chance she'll want to do more.

If she tries to move right into lovemaking, slow her down. Let her know that there's no need to rush. You just want to make her feel good right now. When my partner did this, he'd say, "Uh, uh, uh, not yet. I just want to love your tummy right now." That drove me crazy and made me really want to have sex, even when I wasn't the least bit interested when he first started kissing my belly!

Caressing your wife's belly also sends her a clear message that you love what the two of you are creating together. You are acknowledging how very powerful and sexy it is for her to carry a new life inside of her. This is a great practice to keep up throughout the pregnancy.

Stroking, rubbing, and tickling other nonsexual areas of your partner's body is also very important because in addition to the therapeutic effects, it helps her to stay in touch with her body and the changes she's experiencing. Many women, even this early in their pregnancy, begin to feel as if their bodies are not their own anymore, so pampering her can go a very long way.

For Her

During the first few months of your pregnancy, fatigue, nausea, and emotional roller coasters can smother your sexual desires. While some women are feeling more passionate than ever, others are just not into the idea of having sex right now. No matter which side of this fence you're standing on, you're having a normal reaction. Besides, the way you feel today can easily change by tomorrow. Since your body and mind are interlinked, your mind changes as your body changes and vice versa. Be patient with yourself and be willing to allow yourself the pleasure and closeness that lovemaking with your husband can bring you.

This is also a good time to pamper your partner with other intimate pleasures, ones that don't involve sex. When you have some extra energy, but don't feel turned on, consider treating your man to a soothing manicure or pedicure. (Since you definitely want his fingernails to be trimmed and smoothed to avoid scratching the inside of your vagina, and possibly introducing harmful bacteria, giving him a manicure is a gift for both of you!) He'll feel like a king, and you'll reap your own rewards as a result of this loving gesture. In ancient times, women trained in the arts of lovemaking and seduction often began an erotic encounter by washing their lovers' feet and massaging them with scented oils. Whether you follow the royal foot treatment with sex or not, your husband will be moaning and sighing with pleasure! Another lovely—and probably uncommon—treat for your husband is a candlelit bubble bath. Draw him a hot bath and add a few drops of relaxing essential oil such as lavender or sandalwood. Bubbles are best if they're made from the effervescent of foaming bath salts, rather than the Mr. Bubbles variety that kids love. Those bubbles can be fun for adults, too, but since they're essentially "soap bubbles," they tend to dry adult skin. A fun variation on preparing a tension taming bath for him is to create a sexy bath time experience for both of you!

Draw a warm bath (not hotter than 100 degrees), put a drop or two of lavender in the water, and light a few candles. Floating a few rose petals on the surface of the bath water adds a special touch. As soon as you're in the tub, call for your husband. "Honey, I'm in the tub and I forgot to do something. Can you help me?" When he arrives, invite him into the tub and show him what you forgot to do. . . .

When you feel up for sex, I highly recommend that you introduce something fresh or new every few times. This will accomplish two things: It will keep the passion hot and interesting, which will encourage you both to keep coming back for more; and it will reinforce the foundation of the love affair you're having with each other, triggering memories of your early days together when everything was still new. One very sensual move that men love, and very few women know about, is having their penis stimulated and teased by a woman's hair. As your husband's penis starts to get hard, hold it in your hand and sort of twirl it through your hair. If your hair is too short for twirling, then gently rub your hair back and forth, up and down the head of his penis and around the top of the shaft. This creates an incredibly erotic sensation that is entirely different from your hands, mouth, or tongue.

You can also try the wispy touch of tickling your lover's penis with a feather, or encircling it with a pearl bracelet, and rolling the pearls up and down over the head of his hard-on. Aside from introducing some sexy penis ticklers into your lovemaking, all men love it when you caress their penis with your breasts. This is a huge turn-on for them and can be very exciting for you too. While he watches, massage your breasts and nipples with olive oil, then smooth the oil that's left on your hands all over his penis, starting with the head and working your way down the shaft toward his balls. Once he's erect, and standing at full attention, take the head of the penis and gently rub it around on your breasts. (When you're not pregnant, it feels great to brush it back and forth across your nipples, but they may be too sensitive for that right now.) Instead of having intercourse, bring him to orgasm with your hands, mouth, and other assorted "props," positioning yourself so that he ejaculates on your breasts. Then very seductively, lick just the tiniest drop of his semen off yourself. I assure you that these surprise variations will increase your "sex goddess" self-image, help you to enjoy sex even more, and will most certainly thrill your husband.

Common Questions about the First Trimester:

Q: *Is it okay to douche after sex?*

A: No! Douching after sex is not recommended at any time, but it's definitely a "no-no" during pregnancy. Your body has its own way of cleansing itself. Douching upsets the vagina's natural pH balance and actually puts you at greater risk for a vaginal yeast infection.

Q: *Do we need to use condoms?*

A: That depends. If you were using condoms strictly as a form of birth control, then you're free to ride bareback for the rest of the pregnancy. If, however, you were using condoms to prevent the spread of a sexually transmitted disease, then by all means keep using them. There are certain circumstances, however, when even condoms may not be enough protection. For example, if you are pregnant and you contract herpes simplex II from your partner, you will need to have a Cesarean section. Giving birth vaginally could cause blindness, brain damage, or even death to your baby. So, get all the facts about any disease that you or your partner has and how it can affect your pregnancy.

Q: *Is it safe to use lubricants and massage oils?*

A. As long as they're not petroleum or mineral based, and are pure—meaning there's no preservatives or artificial fragrances—you should be fine. I suggest using olive oil. It's an edible lubricant that doubles as massage oil!

Q: *Is sex in the swimming pool safe at this time?*

A: No, it's not, because the chlorine can cause yeast infections. Not only that, but contrary to what many people believe, water introduced into the vagina during sex does *not* help to lubricate the vagina. It actually dries it out and makes sex more difficult.

Q: *Is it safe to relax or have foreplay in a hot tub or sauna?*

A: No, you should never get in a hot tub or sauna when you're pregnant. Hot tubs and saunas dramatically raise your body temperature and can cause brain damage to your baby. Even hot baths should be avoided. The safe temperature for soaking in the tub is 100 degrees. That's not even two degrees above your normal body temperature, so the water will not feel very warm and it will cool off quickly. If you're looking for heat, I suggest taking a warm shower or sitting next to a crackling fire.

In the next chapter, you'll find out what to expect during the second trimester, learn how to thwart the passion pitfalls, and pick up some spicy-hot lovemaking tips.

Chapter Five

❦

Second Trimester: Hot or Not?

Believe it or not, during the middle three months of your pregnancy, your body will be poised to experience some of the most exciting and satisfying sex that you've ever had or ever will have! Many women say the lovemaking during their second trimester of pregnancy was the best in their entire lives. The same hormones that the body creates in order to grow a healthy baby tend to make women very horny, especially during the middle months of their pregnancy. Of course, not every woman in the second trimester of a pregnancy is "hot to trot" and raring to go, but many women experience a definite lift in their libido.

Most women also feel better, in general, at this time. The nausea and fatigue that may have been a daily part of life in the first trimester often subside or completely vanish in the fourth month of pregnancy. You may also be getting more much-welcomed sleep. Reduced anxiety and a decrease in nocturnal urination can add up to more peaceful nights. Many women feel reenergized during the second trimester and are able to resume most or all of their normal activities. That doesn't mean you should overdo it, but it does mean that you will most likely enjoy these three months much more than the past three! Keep in mind, though, that your baby will grow more during these twelve weeks than during any other trimester, so continue getting proper rest, even when your energy level is high.

In addition to the increased physical comfort during this time, you may also be experiencing greater emotional ease, since the risk of miscarriage is generally over by the end of week twelve.

Sidestepping the Second Trimester's
Top Ten Passion Pitfalls

The expression "Make hay while the sun shines" is fitting for couples who are entering the second trimester. Many women rate the second trimester as their hands-down favorite, not only for sexual pleasure, but also for overall well-being. However, the fact remains that you are growing a baby inside and no matter how good you feel, your body is using a tremendous amount of energy and putting out a terrific effort. In addition to working overtime, 'round the clock your body is experiencing changes that can create unpleasant sensations, ranging from discomfort or annoyance, all the way to real pain. Being aware of what's heading your way gives you an edge. As a couple, you can work together to recognize and sidestep the passion pitfalls and continue growing closer in love.

1. Getting Bigger and Bigger

It's not uncommon for women going into the second trimester to feel bigger, without really looking any bigger. Your abdomen is starting to expand, your breasts are getting fuller, and your hips are beginning to spread. Some women complain that they look "fat" rather than pregnant during months four and five, but by the end of month six, this concern will have disappeared along with your former waistline.

You may feel warmer than usual because as your body works overtime to accomplish its daily goals, it heats up. Drink extra water to cool down and replenish the fluids you're losing through perspiration. Dress in layers, so you can control your body's heating and cooling system throughout the day.

While the physical changes that your body is undergoing may not be getting in the way of sex, the way you and your partner feel about your body's changes can create some passion pitfalls. Some women love it when their tummy starts to round out, and they feel very sexy—even "goddess-like." Other women fear they've lost their youthful sex appeal or worry that their partner will be turned off. It's true that some men view a pregnant woman as anything but sexy, but most men say that when the pregnant woman is their wife, they find her very appealing and sensuous.

Regardless of what side of the fence you're on—"pregnant is sexy" or "pregnant isn't so sexy"—it's reassuring to remember that most of the changes are temporary. It's also a good idea to put a daily practice into place that will help strengthen the bond you have with each other. The closer you feel emotionally, the easier it will be to weather whatever comes your way.

Daily Practice

Love Connection: For thirty seconds, at least twice a day, stand face-to-face with your partner, hold hands, and look into each other's eyes. Silently communicate the love and gratitude you feel for each other, and then share a heart-to-heart hug.

Most couples are really surprised that just one minute a day can make such a dramatic difference in their relationship. The difference occurs because you are tuning in to the love you have for each other. The Love Connection pulls the plug on the rat race, so that for one minute every day, you can really feel each other's love. The baby will feel it too. Some women tell me that their babies often kicked during this exercise. (I tease my male clients by saying, "The Baby can't feel your penis, but it *can* feel your love!)

The Love Connection is definitely a gift you give to yourself and each other at the same time. It sounds so simple that some people blow it off and don't want to bother. But the simplicity is what makes it so powerful and beautiful. This practice will give you both a chance to connect on a deeper level. Both you and your partner will probably be surprised how much love can be shared in just a minute a day. Over days and weeks, the love you feel for each other will most likely override any self-consciousness you are feeling about your body, or any sense of "loss for the old you," that your partner may be experiencing.

2. Morphing into "Mother"

This is where Julia Roberts goes into the doctor's office to take a pregnancy test and, upon learning that the test is positive, turns into Marge Simpson.

Unfortunately, more than a few pregnant women begin mysteriously morphing from "sexy lover" into uptight or "dowdy mother." This role change can happen rapidly or over time, but it can also be avoided, and it must be if you want to continue enjoying your relationship. One of the most damaging things you can do is to take on the stereotypical "good mother" persona. You might be thinking of this as a positive change, but believe me, your mate will undoubtedly translate mother into "my mother." And no husband worth keeping is excited at the thought of having sex with his mother!

Comments from Pregnant Women's Mates

"Four months ago she was prancing around in a black lace teddy and now all she wears are pink flannel nightgowns!"

"She used to be really laid back about the house. Now she's always straightening everything and giving me shit for not putting away my stuff. I swear sometimes she sounds just like my mother."

"Sex used to be awesome with us. Now, she acts like sex is some serious sacred act or something."

"I came home from work and she was in the laundry room unloading the dryer. She had on these baggy sweats, her hair was tied up on top of her head, and she had on face cream. For a second there it was a flashback to my own mom and it really freaked me out."

Get the picture?

Whatever you do, don't fall into the passion pitfall of thinking that once you're pregnant and starting a family, you have to take on a stereotypically more frigid personality. Essentially, you're still the same person. Your hormones will encourage you to "nest," and engage in other "maternal" behaviors, but that doesn't mean that your days of being and feeling sexy are over. On the contrary!

Even though your sex appeal and sexual desires can be yanked around by your hormones, they are also largely a matter of your mind. If you feel unattractive, your sexual self-esteem will go down and you'll be sending out a message that says you're not interested in sexually connecting. If you feel pressure (from yourself or others) to "start acting like a mother," you'll begin to behave in a way that you believe mothers should behave. Traits that are commonly associated with the "good mother" stereotype are nurturing, responsible, warm, patient, levelheaded, and practical. Rarely do people in our society think of traits like "sexy" or "spontaneous" when they're thinking of motherhood. I think we're ready for a change. Why shouldn't mothers be sexy?

Whether you're pregnant or not, or have one child or ten, if you feel sexy, you act sexy. When you're exuding sex appeal, your own desire to make love is often triggered, and you and your partner both get turned on.

3. M-Y Jelly

Now's the time to stock up on panty liners. As your pregnancy progresses, you'll notice that you have more vaginal discharge—sometimes *much* more. These secretions are milky-white in color and have a consistency similar to egg whites. Your pregnancy hormones and increased blood flow to your genitals is creating this discharge and it is normal, albeit a nuisance. If the discharge is any color besides white, or if it has a foul odor, you should check with your doctor. Otherwise, it's simply something to temporarily deal with.

For starters, rather than thinking of it as "discharge," reframe it and think of it as homemade lubricant. It's 100 percent natural and can add a new sensation to your lovemaking for you and your husband. Some couples complain that this puts an end to cunnilingus, but rather than give up something you both love, why not be creative and find a way to work around it? For example, you can take a shower together and wash each other as a part of foreplay. You'll have less "lubricant" right after showering, so that would be a great time for your partner to "go down" on you. If he is leery, let him know that he doesn't have to do a total "muff dive" to get you off. He can stimulate your clitoris and the area around it with his tongue and mouth, without inserting his tongue into your vagina.

4. All Stuffed Up

Well there's not much that's sexy about a stuffy head and postnasal drip, but fortunately this pregnancy symptom usually isn't constant. Many women say that being congested comes and goes, and some women don't experience this condition at all.

When you're not pregnant and you feel congested, you can usually take care of it with an over-the-counter cold remedy. But when you are pregnant, there are often serious risks associated with taking these types of medications. Initially this may seem like a big problem, but if you think about it, we've only had pharmaceutical drugs for the past century or so and women have been having babies for as long as there have been humans. That tells us there must be other ways to deal with this.

Many women say that their congestion was dramatically reduced when they cut back or eliminated dairy products from their diets. However, since dairy products are one of the primary sources of calcium in a North American diet, if you go this route, be sure you get enough calcium from other sources. Some women swear by acupressure, acupuncture, chiropractic treatment, or yoga. Others proclaim the merits of air cleaners, humidifiers, or dehumidifiers. It's definitely worth trying a variety of safe options so you can find out what works the best for you.

If you've been living with a nose that is running one minute and completely clogged the next, you already know that congestion can be a passion pitfall. Stopping between kisses to blow your nose, or fondling your partner with one hand while reaching for a tissue with the other, does have a way of putting a damper on the mood.

Try to keep a sense of humor. A pregnant friend of mine dressed up like a "flapper" with long white gloves for one of her lovemaking sessions. She tucked a handful of tissues into the top of each glove, and, according to her husband, actually managed to make wiping her nose look seductive!

5. Not Tonight, I Have a Headache

One minute you're fine and the next minute you feel like someone just dropped a rock on your head. The unpopular truth is that most women experience some headaches during pregnancy and they often start and stop suddenly. Experts feel that this symptom is caused by the pregnancy hormones, but stress, fatigue, and hunger can trigger one of these headaches as well.

Although you can't totally override the headache response, you can greatly reduce your discomfort by lying down with a cool washcloth on your forehead. If your head is really pounding, try using a bag of frozen peas or corn as an ice pack. It will conform to your head and the cold veggies will shrink the blood vessels and greatly reduce your pain within about fifteen minutes. Another technique that lots of couples swear by is massaging your big toes. Your big toes are the acupuncture points for your head. Squeezing and applying varying amounts of pressure to these toes by massaging and kneading them can bring relief from the headache and considerable pleasure as well.

One husband said, "When my wife used to say she had a headache, that meant no sex. Now when she has a headache, I lay her down on the bed, put an ice pack on her forehead and massage her big toes. Within twenty minutes, her headache is gone and there we both are, on the bed, feeling good. One of the best things I've learned is that a headache can lead to great sex!"

Even so, from the perspective of the person who has the headache, there's nothing like prevention. Consider learning some self-relaxation techniques such as deep breathing, meditation, or calming visualization. If you don't already have a flexibility or gentle stretching routine in place, now is the time to begin one. Tight muscles in your shoulders, neck, and back can result in painful headaches because the blood flow to your head is being constricted.

Another way to keep headaches at bay is to eat several small meals a day and snack on healthy foods to keep your blood sugar level. (See Chapter Four for a list of healthy choices.)

6. Shooting Pains and Seeing Stars

As your uterus gets bigger and heavier, the muscles, ligaments, and tissues that support it have added pressures and more work to accomplish. Your uterus is attached to your pelvis by large ligaments that are called "round ligaments." As your uterus continues to grow, the round ligaments must continue to stretch. Fortunately the elasticity of these ligaments increases slowly and steadily, and the stretching, in itself, is not painful. However, if you make a sudden move, by twisting or turning, getting up, or even sitting down quickly, you may experience a shooting pain on both sides of your pelvis that may even wrap around to your lower back.

Round ligament pain tends to be the worst during the fourth and fifth month of pregnancy. This is when the uterus is big enough to put extra pressure on the ligaments, but not yet big enough to balance some of its weight on your pelvic bones.

To reduce round ligament pain, try to avoid changing positions suddenly. Make a game of it and see how slowly you can stand up from a sitting position. Not only will you avoid the sudden flash of pain, but you'll also be firming up some muscles at the same time. If your old custom was to turn off the alarm clock and go from horizontal to full speed ahead in ten seconds or less, it's time to change your pace. After the alarm goes off, open your eyes and gently stretch your muscles. Make getting out of bed a four-part process—stretch, slowly sit up, put your feet on the floor, and then finally stand up.

If you've been experiencing round ligament pain, the thought of having sex and risking a sudden spontaneous movement, accompanied by excruciating pain, probably doesn't sound very appealing. Unfortunately, most men are not very sympathetic in this symptom department, because they simply don't understand how a ligament that isn't actually injured could cause so much distress. Give your partner a break, and chalk it up to the reality that there's really no way that he can totally understand what you're experiencing. While this may be upsetting to you, it can actually be more upsetting for him. Many men say that some of the hardest things about their wives' pregnancies were feeling left out, not really being able to understand what she was going through, and not knowing what they could do to make her feel better.

Meanwhile, there *are* ways to get around the potential passion pitfall. Here's what to do: Ask your husband to gently massage your sides and lower back with warm olive oil as you sit in bed, propped up against a mountain of fluffy pillows. As you relax into the pleasing sensations, your husband can massage his way down around your belly and move to your inner thighs. You will be in the perfect position to gratefully enjoy oral sex, and by slowing turning over onto your hands and knees, you can have intercourse. Rather than moving your entire upper body to and fro, gently rock your hips back and forth, while keeping the rest of your body relatively still. This is a win-win scenario for you and your partner, and your baby will probably enjoy the gentle rocking as well.

7. Tightness and Tension

Muscle tightness and tension can be a passion pitfall at any time, but it can become a real "pain in the neck" when you're pregnant. Fortunately, this is another potential pitfall that can be turned to your favor. In today's busy world everyone could benefit by bodywork, such as massage and chiropractic treatment, and also by stretching more and tensing less.

If your budget will permit it, have a licensed massage therapist come to your home once a month to give both you and your partner a massage. Getting a massage at home is one of life's greatest luxuries! When the massage is finished and you're lying there feeling like you now know what nirvana means, you can just keep on lying there. You don't have to get up, get dressed, and then drive home, often undoing a lot of the good that was done. (Massage gift certificates are wonderful to give and receive. If friends or family members are looking for gift ideas, I'd put massage near the top of the list!)

Meanwhile, whether you're getting professionally massaged or not, I highly recommend giving each other massages at least once a week. If you and your mate haven't invested in a good instructional massage book or video, what are you waiting for? I know I've mentioned it before, but it's worth stressing because giving each other massages is one of the most generous, intimate, and healing ways that you can express your love and concern for one another. It's also a great prelude to lovemaking and the ultimate grand finale as well.

8. Dryness and Itching

Did you know that when skin stretches, it itches? If you didn't know before, chances are that you know now. Many pregnant women suffer from dry skin and feel itchy all over. Lotions and oils will soothe your skin and give you some relief, but they can only do so much and they need to be applied frequently to keep working.

Invest in a safe, natural oil or lotion to keep on hand, but don't stop there. You can alleviate some of the itching from the inside out, by drinking plenty of pure water every day. (The general rule of thumb is 64 ounces a day. However, to get a more accurate assessment of the amount of water you need each day, divide your weight by two. The result is the minimum number of ounces you should drink each day, and since you're pregnant it's a good idea to add another 8 or 12 ounces to that number.)

Some women also say that humidifying the air in their homes makes a significant difference in alleviating dry skin, especially in colder climates where indoor heating can quickly pull moisture out of the air. It's important to note that increasing your water intake and adding water to the air can relieve dry skin, but swimming and taking baths and showers actually reduces the moisture in your skin. Even though soaking in a tub or standing in a warm shower may feel great on your skin while you're in there, the longer you bathe, the more you will pay the price when you dry off. Taking shorter showers and baths will help your skin to maintain its moisture, and applying lotion, cream, or oil will help to seal your skin and keep the moisture in.

Many women find it very erotic for their partners to rub them with warm oil, and it's no surprise that this can be a perfect prelude to great sex.

9. Pelvic Cramps

As early as the fifth month of pregnancy, you may begin to have cramps from time to time that feel a lot like menstrual cramps. These cramps are actually mini-contractions (sometimes called "Braxton Hicks contractions"), and while the idea of having contractions in the second trimester may sound alarming, in this case it's actually a good sign. These miniature contractions are your body's way of exercising and preparing for the full contractions that will occur when your baby is due.

Pelvic cramps generally do not occur while you're having sex, although it wouldn't be surprising to have it happen from time to time. What is common, however, is having these mini-contractions in conjunction with an orgasm. This is not at all harmful to the mother or the baby, but it can be frightening if you don't know what's going on. Basically, as a result of the orgasm, the pelvic floor muscles contract and tighten and pull all the other surrounding muscles tight. Your belly will feel hard and tight, but it will relax and return to its softer, more supple state within a few moments.

The reason pelvic cramps and mini-contractions can be a passion pitfall is that many women and men misinterpret them by thinking they are a "bad" thing, rather than something that is both "good" and expected. If you or your mate is uncomfortable about making love because of your pelvic cramps, it's a good idea for both of you to talk with your doctor and address your fears and concerns about what's happening. He or she will be able to answer your questions, and if everything is okay (it most likely is) your minds will be at ease and you can jump this passion pitfall!

Meanwhile, these contractions can feel surprisingly strong, especially for a woman who has never experienced a full-blown contraction. This is another physical sensation that men have a hard time understanding. It was summed up beautifully on a *Friends* episode after Rachel, who was several months pregnant, went to the doctor because she was having pains in her abdomen. The father of her baby, Ross, casually said, "Oh yeah. Braxton Hicks contractions. Those are nothing." To which Rachel curtly replied, "No uterus. No opinion!"

10. Pains in the Butt

If you still don't know what a hemorrhoid feels like, count yourself among the fortunate few. By the end of this trimester, hemorrhoids tend to be common complaints. Everyone knows that hemorrhoids are a pain in the butt, but you may not know that they are actually varicose veins. If you have varicose veins in your legs, you already know how painful they can be. Having these swollen veins in your rectum will cause even greater discomfort, and sometimes cause rectal bleeding.

Pregnant women are most susceptible to hemorrhoids because they have high levels of the hormone progesterone, which affects the veins in the anal canal. Straining during a bowel movement can also cause these swollen pouches, so by all means, get enough roughage and drink enough water. Regular exercise helps to make elimination a smoother process, and such exercises as walking, running, and stair-stepping massage the intestines and can greatly reduce constipation.

If you develop hemorrhoids, you can relieve some of the pain and itching by gently washing your rectum after each bowel movement. I recommend using a soft cloth or prepackaged witch-hazel pads. Another safe and soothing treatment is Aloe Vera gel. Don't bother with the stuff that comes prepackaged. It often has additives, and the live properties of the plant have long been dead. Buy a few Aloe Vera plants and keep one in your bathroom along with a paring knife. When you're having a bout with hemorrhoids, cut off one of the plant's leaves. (The plant will rather miraculously seal its own cut.) Just one Aloe leaf can last several days because you only use about an inch at a time. Take the leaf that you have cut from the plant, and slice off a 1- or 2-inch piece. Some Aloe plants have tiny spikes about every inch or so along both edges of the leaf. If your leaf has these minuscule thorns, be sure to carefully prune them off. Next, take the section you have cut, and slice the green "skin" off one side of the leaf, exposing the healing gel within. Place the gel side of the leaf section directly on the hemorrhoid, and hold it in place until the cool sensation subsides.

Rectal pain doesn't have to be a total passion pitfall, but it often is because so many women are embarrassed to tell their partners that they have hemorrhoids. Discussing protrusions in your rectum is not exactly a turn-on, but it's better to be honest than to reject your partner's advances without explaining why. If you let him know what's going on, it will be easier for both of you. Instead of just saying "no," reach a happy medium, with some sort of compromise to be played out either now or later when you're feeling better.

For those of you who enjoy anal sex, I can assure you that hemorrhoids will nip that pleasure in the bud! Even women who couldn't get enough rear action before will probably choose to designate this erogenous zone as an "exit only"—at least until after the baby is born.

CHART 5.1   WHAT'S GOING ON INSIDE?

Second Trimester

MONTH FOUR

- By the time you are four months' pregnant, your uterus is about the size of a grapefruit. You can feel it between your belly button and your pubic bone.
- During the fourth month, your baby doubles in length and more than triples in weight. He or she is now approximately 3 to 5 inches long and weighs about 2 ounces.
- Your baby's legs begin to lengthen and he or she may start kicking, but you probably won't feel it yet.
- Your baby can now flex its arms, clasp its hands, and suck its thumb. He or she is now floating freely and safely in the amniotic sac.

MONTH FIVE

- By now, your baby's outer ears are developing and so is his or her hearing.
- If you haven't already felt your baby move, it could happen any day now. Many women describe these movements as flutters, or ripples.
- Your baby's legs are now about as big as your little fingers. If you haven't felt a kick yet, you soon will.
- At the end of five months, your baby is about 8 to 10 inches long and weighs about a half pound. He or she is also able to hear sounds now.

MONTH SIX

- Your baby weighs almost a pound, and is about the size of a small doll.
- Your baby's eyebrows and eyelids are now well developed.
- You may begin to feel full-fledged kicking that is strong enough that your partner will probably be able to feel it too.
- Your baby has fully developed fingernails and eyelashes. Air sacs are beginning to develop in the lungs.
- By the end of the second trimester, your baby weighs about 2 pounds and is about 1 foot long.

Tips and Techniques for the
Second Trimester

Many men find the growing roundness of their pregnant partner's body very sexy and erotic. However, it's not uncommon for a man to be somewhat unnerved as he watches his lover's body change so dramatically. It's also not unusual for a man to begin feeling left out or to start withdrawing because of emotional turmoil about the role change and added responsibilities of being a father.

Whether your husband is really into the changes that are occurring, or not, it is equally important to keep your sexual connection strong at this time. Remember that sharing and enjoying the intimacy and passion of sex are essential if you want to continue to be each other's lovers throughout the pregnancy and after the baby is born.

Don't wait for your partner to initiate sex, or you will find yourself in a frustrating and potentially no-win situation. There are many reasons why the same man who couldn't get enough a few months ago will stop playing the role of Romeo. He may be trying to respect your space, or perhaps he just feels a little uncomfortable. In some cases, men still think of pregnant women as being "off limits." This may seem ridiculous to a modern-day woman, but remember that for hundreds of thousands of years there have been powerful taboos and inaccurate assumptions surrounding the mystery and physical manifestation of pregnancy and childbirth. Chances are that both you and your partner are still being affected in some ways by these old and mistaken ideas, so rather than getting upset with each other, get naked, get on with it, and get over it!

During the next three to four months, there will be times when you feel incredibly alive and sexier than you have ever felt before. Take full advantage of these times to enjoy some awesome sex and treat your partner to your hormone-heightened passion.

Meanwhile, even though the physical changes can throw you for a loop, most couples actually have a greater challenge dealing with the emotional turbulence that pregnancy tends to create. Since sex begins outside of the bedroom, whatever is happening or not happening in the rest of your relationship is going to have a big impact on your sex life. It's more important than ever to tactfully air your grievances and problem solve together. Work together, play together, and stay together!

The Right Angles

While you were able to enjoy any sexual position you desired during the first trimester, it will now be important to make a few modifications. To begin with, after the fourth month, it's recommended that you stop having sex in the missionary position, because it is no longer safe for a woman to lie on her back. An artery that runs the length of the spine is primarily responsible for getting blood to the fetus. When a woman is lying on her back, she can theoretically slow or stop the fetus's blood supply. The best position for a woman to lie in from this point until the end of the pregnancy is on her left side with a pillow under her belly.

If you want to have intercourse while lying down, prop your right leg up on a few pillows so that your partner can enter you from behind. This is also a prime position for receiving oral sex!

If you and your partner are fond of the "woman on top" position, get it out of your system during the fourth month, because it's not a good idea after that. When the woman is on top after the fifth month of pregnancy, she runs the risk of doing painful and possibly permanent damage to her hips and knees.

Avoid both the missionary position and the woman-on-top position from month five on. Because these tend to be the most commonly used positions, this is a chance to try some new things and begin branching out. Variety really can be the spice of sex, so use your pregnancy to be more creative and innovative in your lovemaking.

One of the safest and easiest positions is "doggie style." Though the name isn't much of a turn-on, this position is comfortable for both the man and the woman and allows easy access to the vagina. Your husband will also have his hands free to fondle your breasts, stroke the area around the clitoris, or hold on to your hips as he thrusts. This is also a position very conducive to stimulating a woman's "G spot." The G spot is a small area located a few inches inside the vagina. It's on the front-facing wall of a woman's vagina, and if it is directly rubbed with the head of a penis (or when you're not pregnant, a dildo or vibrator), the sensations can erupt into a breathtaking, knee-shaking sort of orgasm. Experiment with different angles of entry and tell each other what feels the best.

An amusing pastime for pregnant couples is taking a tour of your home, looking at each counter and chair as you've never looked at them before. The idea is to identify the furniture that will be most conducive to sex, now that lying on your back or being on top are no longer options. For example, the overstuffed recliner in the sunroom could become the perfect "sex chair." Or maybe you'll find that by sitting on the edge of your kitchen table (on a pillow or two) your mate can enter you while he's standing up. If it's oral sex you want, he can simply pull up a chair and "voila"!

When it's your turn to repay the favor, simply switch positions. You'll be surprised just how many different pieces of furniture are "sex-friendly." Just be sure that you have the proper support and stability to be safe before you get into it!

For Him

Now's the time for you to step up to the plate and knock in a few runs, and I don't mean in the bedroom. Many pregnant women begin to feel somewhat overwhelmed during the second trimester, so the more you can do to help lighten her load, the better it will be for all three of you (or more if you already have other children). Besides that, on a very practical and realistic note, the more you do to help your mate, the more energy she'll have left for lovemaking, and the more she'll want to be intimate with you. So, go for the win-win situation!

Aside from picking up the dry cleaning, having dinner delivered, and doing various other sundry errands, there's something very special that you can do to support your wife, and I guarantee that you'll both love it!

Ready? There's an exercise that you and your wife can do together that will help to make the birth of your baby easier. It's called the "Kegel" (named after the doctor who invented it), and it tones and strengthens a woman's pelvic-floor muscles. Generally, women are instructed to do this exercise alone, but I think that once they understand how it works, it's much more fun to do as a couple.

Before you practice my altered version of the Kegel, it will be important for your wife to do a few on her own, so she can identify and isolate the inner muscles that she is going to be working with. She should begin by practicing the stopping and releasing of her urine flow several times when she urinates. By doing this, she will learn which muscles are the pelvic floor muscles and how to contract and release them at will.

Step two (and this is where you come in [literally perhaps]) is for her to practice this same exercise with your penis inside her. You will need to stay relatively still, which drives most men crazy. Once she completes a few sets of Kegels, what happens next is up to the two of you. So far, every man I've shared this with has reported great results. It gives you a chance to sexually connect with your partner while at the same time helping her to strengthen the muscles that will make her delivery easier. Not only that, but you will master the art of better control, and consequently become an even better lover.

Naturally, the more proficient you are as a lover, the more enthusiastic your wife will be about making love. Something that you may not know is that most women report greater pleasure from a low-intensity orgasm achieved during lovemaking with their mates than from a high-intensity climax that they achieve by masturbating. Since women generally place a high value on the bonding and sharing aspects of sex, it makes sense that their greatest enjoyment occurs when they are with their mates. A husband who has a desire to please his wife can actually give her more pleasure and sexual fulfillment than she can give to herself. That's a very sexy and powerful position to be in! When you add to that your commitment to love and cherish her, both inside the bedroom and out, you are creating the magic flames that will keep your love affair glowing long after your kids have grown up and started families of their own.

Okay, now that your motor is starting to rev, let me cool you back down with a practical, commonsense caution. Many, many women get upset with their husbands during pregnancy because these mature, grown men suddenly turn into moping, whining, passive-aggressive five-year-olds when their wives say no to their sexual advances. Do your wife and your self-respect a favor and don't behave like this! It won't get you an inch closer to getting what you want. And if your wife does give in just to "appease you" or "shut you up" (yes, women *do* say things like this) I guarantee the pleasure will not be worth the longer-term cost.

Being an award-winning lover isn't based solely on your technical skills or sexual performance. The best lovers are making love to their wives all the time, in a thousand different ways that extend into every facet of marriage. If you haven't been taking the initiative to plan romantic dates and outings with your partner, you're dropping the ball on one of the most important aspects of being a great lover. Why shoot yourself in the foot when it's so easy to pick up the phone and make a dinner reservation?

Another way to score big points in your wife's heart is to write her some love notes and place them strategically around the house, or in her office and car. Those sticky note pads work great for this purpose. You can write compliments, tell her why you love her so much, or why you're so proud of her. Tell her how sexy and beautiful she is. I also recommend thanking her for whatever you are most grateful for about her and your marriage. Each little note can be a simple one-liner from your heart. She will treasure each one of them and brag about you to her friends.

Another way to romance your pregnant partner is to send her a gift at her office or place of employment. (If she's at home, send the gift through the mail or have it delivered.) Everyone loves to receive a gift and when a man gives a woman a gift, just to say, "I love you," or "I adore you," that rates right up there with back rubs and orgasms! Flowers and plants are nearly always welcome gifts, so are gift baskets or a book or CD that she's been wanting. Other great gifts for a woman in her second trimester are a lumbar support pillow for her office chair or car seat, a foot stool to elevate her feet while she's sitting, or an aroma-therapy neck support pillow. The ones you can heat up in a microwave are really great. The heat is very soothing on her tense neck muscles, and the scent is calming. Caring enough to surprise her with something thoughtful is a very loving way to show her that she means the world to you. Gestures like these warm the heart and affirm the spirit of your love for her.

For Her

Now's the perfect time to start finding out what your body can really do. Since your vagina is engorged with blood, technically, your body is in a state of semi-arousal twenty-four hours a day, even if having sex is the furthest thing from your mind. The beauty of this is that when your thoughts or fantasies do turn to sex, it doesn't take long before you're feeling aroused and ready for love. And believe me, the lovemaking can be outstanding if you take your time and really let the sensations in your body carry you away. I encourage you to embrace your inner sex goddess and get really good at seducing your husband. If you have any fear of failure with this, let me assure you that it won't be hard to do! Most men don't actually have to be seduced, and since your husband will automatically be a willing participant, the idea of seduction isn't to "talk him into sex," but rather to make him want you so much that he'll get down on his knees and beg you for it.

The ability to play the seductress in this way with your husband is one of the most important aspects of being an exceptional lover. It's also one of the most effective ways to retain your role of "lover," once you become a mother. I'm not suggesting that you do this every time, but doing it every now and again increases the intensity of his desire and yours. The objective is to stretch out the amount of time between giving him a hard-on and bringing him to orgasm. One of the most reliable aspects of the penis is that it points a man toward intercourse the way a compass points to the north. I imagine it's a way to ensure the continuation of the human race! In any case, it's your job to slow him down and keep him aroused simultaneously. Once he has an orgasm, sex is pretty much over for him, so the longer he gets to experience pleasure before he climaxes, the more intense, powerful, and satisfying his orgasm will be.

A very playful and enticing way to begin an afternoon of seduction is to bend over and let him see the red lace pregnancy thong that you're wearing under your skirt. Next, unbutton your blouse down to your waist and kiss him on the back of his neck. Be creative about how all the clothes come off, because once you're married, getting undressed tends to lose most of its electricity. Bring the sparks back by undressing him a little at a time. Or pretend to be ignoring him as your own clothing mysteriously disappears, one garment at a time. If your husband is a card player, challenge him to a game of strip poker. There's something very enticing and rather naughty about gambling each other's clothes off at the kitchen table!

This is also an opportune time to introduce some new scenarios into your love play. Once your husband's clothes are all off and lying about on the floor, use your bra or his tie to bind his hands loosely together behind his chair. Position yourself on a pillow at his feet and gently spread his legs and take his penis into your hands. One of the most erotic forms of variety in performing fellatio involves teasing the penis and heightening its sense of touch by alternating the temperature surrounding his penis from warm to cold to warm again. The most efficient way to accomplish this is in your mouth. Get two mugs and fill one of them with ice water and the other with very warm water or tea. Test the heated water to be sure that it feels warmer than your mouth, but plenty cool enough not to burn. Once your lover is erect, take a sip of the warm water and hold it in your mouth and as you slide his penis into your mouth, enveloping it in a pool of warm water. Swallow the water, and continue stroking his penis with your hand while you take a sip of ice water. This time, hold the water in your mouth for a few seconds and swallow it before you use your cool tongue and mouth on him. Some guys love it when you keep the ice water in your mouth along with their penis, but for some men this sensation is too much. Where sex is concerned, it's usually smarter to start with more moderate variations of what you're accustomed to and increase your intensity and variety a step or two at a time.

Aside from bringing your husband and yourself to new heights of passion and pleasure, it's also very important to be loving to your mate throughout your day-to-day interactions. Be the catalyst in creating a loving atmosphere that will nurture the physical and emotional growth and development of your marriage as well as your baby. And, when things are not going the way you want them to go, remember that you catch more bears with honey than with vinegar! Don't dwell on what your husband's *not* doing or what he's doing *wrong*. Give him positive feedback on what he *is* doing to help you and tell him how much you appreciate it. Showing and telling your partner how much you love him and how important he is to you and your growing family will help him to dissolve some of the fears and anxieties that he may not know how to deal with.

One more thing, if your mate didn't read the bit above about the Kegel exercises, read it to him and schedule your first workout session!

In Chapter Six, find out how to maneuver around the third trimester's top ten romance roadblocks and learn more tips and techniques to keep your intimacy strong, even when sex is out of the question!

Chapter Six

Third Trimester: Sex Is Best When You Nest—But Get Your Rest

Less than a hundred years ago in many parts of the world, even the "thought" of having sex when a woman was "with child" was considered perverse. Actually *doing* the deed—especially after a woman was "showing"—would have been considered the height of deviant behavior. Aside from being taboo, up until recently many doctors believed that women should abstain from sexual intercourse during the final trimester of pregnancy for fear of hurting the baby or prematurely inducing labor.

Thank goodness all of that has changed! Most doctors now agree that if your pregnancy is normal and healthy, you can continue enjoying sexual intercourse and having orgasms right up until you go into labor. Of course, whether or not you feel up to it is another thing. Most likely, you are feeling huge, clumsy, and exhausted. Your back hurts, your feet are swelling, and you can't walk up a flight of stairs without feeling winded. Needless to say, the frequency of sex play tends to take a nose dive at this point. Speaking from experience (having had two babies of my own), I know there are days and even weeks at a time when the last thing in the world a pregnant woman wants to do is have sex. That's completely understandable. But there's another side to this coin.

Having an orgasm is one of the best ways for your body to release tension and relax into a peaceful sleep. Not only that, but the hormones that are created through lovemaking help you and your partner feel an increased sense of security and courage. Your baby will be positively affected by these hormones, too, and may even decide to take a little nap of his or her own. Some doctors believe that having sex throughout the third trimester can help to smooth the way for the delivery.

Another important reason to engage in lovemaking at this time is to intimately connect with your partner. Many pregnant women's husbands feel more rejected and abandoned during the last few months and weeks before childbirth. A woman who is soon to deliver has a tendency to turn inward, and many men experience this as being "pushed out." There is really no way for you to verbalize exactly what you are feeling and sensing, and your husband knows that no matter how much he loves you, this is an experience that he can only take part in *through* you. For this reason, making love together, at least occasionally, is very important now. When you are too tired or preoccupied to make love to him with your body, make it a point to make love to him with your eyes and by rubbing his neck when you stand behind him, or reaching for and squeezing his hand when you're watching television. Some communication specialists estimate that more than 80 percent of our essential communication takes place on a nonverbal level. What that basically means is that we can fulfill each other's basic relationship needs of love and gratitude without speaking. But we can't fulfill these needs without our bodies and our gestures. There are good reasons for sayings like "Actions speak louder than words" and "Words are cheap." For two people to stay lovers, actions are often more valuable than words.

No one, including yourself, should expect you to have sex when you're too tired or just don't want to for whatever reason. It can be worthwhile, however, for you to plan some special times to cuddle up with your partner and at least be open to the idea of sex. Look at your calendar and pick a day when you can really relax and pamper yourself, rather than trying to fit it in at the end of a long day of work or errands.

If your mate is smart, he'll plan special pamper days for you. A caring partner will want to help his wife feel better and do what he can for her at this time—but it's up to you to let him know what you need and how he can help. Even though your needs most certainly come first right now, remember that your lover still has needs, too, and one of them is knowing that you value and appreciate him. Don't wait until you're "in the mood" to show him how much you care. Create the mood, and you'll both benefit.

Dodging the Third Trimester's Top Ten Romance Roadblocks

Even though you *do* want to make love, there are lots of physical challenges that can get in the way, the most obvious being your belly. The following are some suggestions for how to get around the conditions that can become roadblocks to your romance.

1.   Heart-Pounding Messages

By the time you are in your seventh month of pregnancy, your body has 45 percent more blood than it did when you became pregnant. That means your heart is working harder to pump the extra blood and your heart rate has probably increased by about 10 beats per minute. Obviously, the more physically fit you are, the easier it is for your heart to adjust to the added demands.

Many women feel their heart pounding when they exercise, have sex, or stand up suddenly. This is a message from your body letting you know that your heart is working too hard and you need to slow or stop what you are doing. Since you know that this is a condition that you need to be aware of, it's better to plan ahead where sex is concerned. For the most part, your partner is going to be doing most of the "work," for the time being. By reducing the amount of your own movements, you give your heart a break, but can still give yourself and your mate a pleasurable experience. Fortunately, within a few weeks after giving birth, as your circulatory system returns to its pre-pregnant state, these heart-pounding sensations will stop.

2.   You Take My Breath Away

While you may feel short of breath, you are actually taking in more air with each breath than you did before you were pregnant. Pregnancy causes your respiratory system to go through amazing changes so that you are able to take in the extra oxygen needed to breathe for you and your baby. Your ability to take in more air with each breath increases, and some women's rib cages even expand by an inch or two. So why do you sometimes feel like you can't catch your breath?

Basically that's because you don't have as much room for your lungs to expand to their full capacity. During the last few months of pregnancy, your diaphragm (the broad, flat muscle that is underneath your lungs) is pushed an inch or so out of place by your growing uterus. In order to compensate for the lack of space, pregnancy hormones stimulate your respiratory system to breathe more often and more efficiently. This ensures that both you and the baby get the oxygen you need.

Fortunately, your feelings of breathlessness do not mean that your baby is actually lacking oxygen. Just knowing this helps some women to relax enough to breathe more easily. As long as your episodes of breathlessness are infrequent, and you can improve your breathing by standing or sitting up straight, there's no need to worry. (If you have a sudden, severe shortness of breath, along with a rapid pulse or chest pain, you should seek immediate medical care because this could be a sign of a serious problem.)

When you're not pregnant, you want sex to be so great that it leaves you breathless, but now that same feeling can cause anxiety and discomfort. For this reason, many women favor having intercourse while sitting up. This position allows your best lung capacity, and by supporting your lower back with pillows, you will probably feel very comfortable.

3.   Puffy Hands and Swollen Feet

By the end of your pregnancy, you're carrying around an extra 2 to 3 gallons of fluid, so swollen hands, legs, and feet are par for the course. You will tend to have the most swelling in areas where gravity causes fluid to settle. As long as elevating your legs and feet for an hour or so makes the swelling go down, you are probably experiencing "gravity edema."

Some women mistakenly believe that the swelling means they are drinking too much water and they reduce their intake. Do not do this! The truth is that you probably need more fluid than you are currently drinking. Your pregnancy hormones cause you to feel thirsty so that you will drink more water. Your body uses the extra fluid to take care of your baby's fluid needs as well as refill the amniotic fluid pool. Extra water is also needed to increase the water level in your blood so that your kidneys can wash away waste more efficiently. Your urine should be almost colorless or only slightly yellow. If it is darker, you are probably not drinking enough water and you may be dehydrated.

If the swelling in your feet or legs seems extreme, take the "press test." Press your finger down into a swollen area for a second or so. If your finger leaves an obvious indentation, you may have "pitting edema." Another sign of this form of edema is if the swelling does not go down after elevating your feet for an hour. In this case, your body might be telling you that there is a problem and you should seek medical attention. Fluid retention that is excessive or builds up very quickly can be a sign of more serious conditions such as preeclampsia or toxemia.

Try not to sit or stand for more than an hour at a time. If you absolutely have to stand for extended periods of time for your job, try to take a three- to five-minute break every thirty minutes to put your feet up. Don't cross your legs when you sit because this restricts circulation and can increase swelling. Be sure to elevate your feet at the end of every day for at least an hour and preferably several times a day.

Walking, swimming, riding a stationary bike, and making love are all excellent for increasing circulation. Plus having sex can be done in a horizontal position, which means that you can "put your feet up" at the same time. I recommend putting on some sexy lingerie and reclining on your bed or sofa, while your mate gently rubs your feet and calves with warm oil. As you begin to relax, he can slowly move his efforts upward, and you can join in at any time.

4.   Oh My Aching Back!

At least half of all pregnant women experience some degree of back pain during the last few months of pregnancy. By design, your ligaments are relaxing so that your baby will have a more flexible passage through the pelvis. However, this puts more strain on your muscles—especially the ones that support your spine. Your back muscles are also picking up the slack for your stretched abdominal muscles, forcing you to rely on your back to support most of your weight. Add to that the fact that by now your are "front heavy," and the result is, "Oh, my aching back!"

The best way to deal with backaches is to prevent them by strengthening and toning the muscles in your back and abdomen. If you start doing this now, by the time you reach the third trimester you will be really glad you did! Even gaining a little extra strength in your back muscles will make a big difference when you get down to the last month or two of your pregnancy.

Aerobic exercises, such as swimming, stair-stepping, and cycling, will also help to strengthen your lower back and abdominal muscles. If you have a walking or running routine that typically puts you on hard surfaces, for example, asphalt or concrete, make it a point to find another route with more natural surfaces, such as grass, mulch, dirt, or sand. If you live in an area where natural surfaces are few and far between, find out about running tracks in the vicinity. Many high schools and colleges have outdoor running tracks that are made from special surfaces designed to cushion your landing. A nearby health club or training facility may have an indoor running track (an added perk if it's raining or cold outside).

Avoid high heels and flats. Try shoes with wide, stable heels (no more than 2 inches) and plenty of arch support. If you are among the majority of women whose feet expand during pregnancy, invest in the highest quality shoes that you can afford. Get at least one pair of great walking shoes and a pair of comfortable, supportive dress shoes. Your feet have acupuncture points that correspond with every part of your body, and they are your primary "foundation." Even though your feet may return to their previous size, and your "pregnancy shoes" will only get a few months' wear, quality shoes are a must.

Another thing to be aware of is your body posture, because certain movements can increase back pain. For starters, try to avoid twisting your spine, and don't try to twist and lift at the same time. While you're sitting or standing, keep your pelvis tucked in and your shoulders back. Before you stand up or sit down, make sure your hips and shoulders are aligned.

Take the stress off your lower back by lying down on your left side with a pillow supporting your abdomen and another one between your knees. You are now in a prime position for lovemaking and you may be pleased to learn that the feel-good hormones created by having sex and climaxing can temporarily flood your body with painkillers. The painkillers your body makes naturally are the best for you and your baby because they are absolutely safe and healthy. You can even gently stretch your lower back when having sex, by gently tilting your pelvis up and forward and then out and back. Both you and your mate will like this "pelvis tilt" and will want to keep it in your repertoire even after the baby is born.

5.   Loose Hips

During the last trimester many women feel a sense of discomfort in their hips and pubic bone, especially when they're walking. This happens because all of the ligaments in the vicinity of your pelvis are stretching and your cartilage is actually softening in preparation for the birth of your baby. Your hips are literally loosening up, which is why your walk feels more like a waddle these days.

It's also why the "woman on top" position should be removed from your possibilities, if it hasn't been nixed already. Although both women and men often favor this position in the late stages of pregnancy, it can do a lot of lasting damage to a woman's knees and hips. It can also potentially increase the discomfort in your hips.

6.   Minihiccups

Right around the seventh month, you may begin to feel your baby's hiccups. Fetal hiccups are common during the second half of a pregnancy and often are more frequent in the final trimester. The experts agree that they're nothing to worry about, but there's very little clear explanation for why they occur. Some women report that their babies had a pattern of hiccuping at a certain time each day. Other women say that eating certain foods seemed to trigger the baby's hiccups.

For you, the hiccups will feel a little like there's a small balloon in your belly that suddenly expands, and then contracts again. They don't hurt, they just feel rather odd, and definitely different from kicks and punches. They generally come and go quickly, but they can last as long as twenty minutes or so.

You may be surprised to hear that many couples report that fetal hiccups are one of the most prevalent romance roadblocks in the eighth and ninth month of pregnancy. One woman said, "We were having this great lovemaking session, and all of a sudden the baby started to hiccup. I tried to focus on my husband and what he was doing, but I just got fixated on those hiccups and it went downhill from there." Some couples also believe that if the baby has hiccups while they're having sex that it's a sign that the baby is disturbed or upset. There is absolutely no evidence of this, and I am firm believer that the more you and your mate enjoy each other, the more enjoyable the pregnancy will be for your baby and the more secure he or she will feel after birth.

7. Sparring and Kick Boxing

During the seventh month of your pregnancy, you're likely to feel as if your uterus is a boxing ring. Most women report the greatest amount of punching and kicking during this month, and many of them are surprised, but proud, of just how big a punch their little one can pack. Some women worry that the intensity of the jabs and kicks will be too much to take if the baby keeps getting stronger, but that's not likely to happen. It seems that during the seventh month your baby's arms and legs are long and strong enough to make their mark, and at the same time, there is still enough extra space in the womb for an ample windup before the pitch! However, these acrobatics will be greatly reduced in the months to come.

During months eight and nine, the kicks and punches tend to be much less frequent, but they can still hurt! Most of the sensations you have felt up to this point are probably coming from one specific place in the womb where baby is pushing out a fist or kicking or stretching a leg. Now you can feel the baby in several places at the same time. You may feel a foot pushing up under one of your ribs and the pressure of the baby's head or shoulders in your pelvis at the same time.

Regardless of how precious feeling your baby move really is to you, getting a swift kick in the ribs while you're making love usually doesn't add to your sexual excitement. But it doesn't have to put an end to what you're doing either. After all, once this little one is born there are going to be plenty of untimely interruptions in your lovemaking. Now's the time to learn how to "take five," and then resume play!

8. Feeling Huge

Just when you feel like there's no way that you can function if you get any bigger, the growing stops. Once you make it to the eighth month, you've probably reached your peak and will hold steady until the end of your term. Once the baby begins to drop lower into your pelvis, you will have more room under your ribs again, and some women say this makes them feel a little smaller. Other women say that when the baby moved down they actually felt even bigger, even though they may not have looked bigger.

Most women agree that the "huge and awkward" stage is anything but sexy or glamorous. Such simple tasks as tying your own shoes or retrieving the dish detergent from under the sink become daring acrobatic feats. Basic abilities that you mastered long ago, such as walking through a doorway without hitting either side of the frame, will suddenly elude you. It's as if your body has changed dimensions too rapidly for your mind to comprehend it—like getting used to driving a truck when you've had a sports car your whole life.

You really need to be more careful and also to give yourself a break. Remember that you have actually lost (temporarily) your normal agility and coordination in your hands and your feet. Rather than spontaneously jumping into something, it will be necessary for you to think it through before you take action. "Look before you leap" would be a good motto right now and "Stop before you step" would be even better.

Probably the most comforting thing for you to remember is the obvious: This is temporary and you are entering the final stretch!

Meanwhile, you may be pleasantly surprised to discover that your mate is really turned on by your body in "full bloom." A lot of men find this incredibly erotic, but many of them are too afraid or repressed to show it, especially since the taboos still linger in the minds of many. It may be up to you to initiate lovemaking now, and I strongly urge you to do it. When you are near the end of your pregnancy, your genitals are engorged with blood and you are literally bursting with life. Feeling the sensation of your lover's penis inside of you can feel almost other-worldly. The actual sensations are different for every couple, but the comments have a common theme: "Wow! I never dreamed it could feel like that!"

9.   Sheer Exhaustion

During the last couple months of your pregnancy, your body will be burning up so much fuel to complete the major job of creating a healthy baby that there will be very little gas left in the tank for anything else. There's really nothing you can or should do about this, except honor and respect it. If you push yourself too hard, you end up paying the price in double, plus interest. It's just not worth trying to go against the flow at this point. Now's a good time to refresh your memory on children's songs like *Row, Row, Row Your Boat.* Notice that it says "gently *down* the stream," not vigorously against the current! (Sometimes there's surprising wisdom in children's rhymes and games.)

Some women report that during the last month or so they feel so tired that everything they do takes a tremendous amount of effort. Please listen to your body. Even though you may have sailed through these months in previous pregnancies, if your body is telling you it needs rest, it needs rest!

Plan a restful evening together with your mate. Have your dinner delivered, watch a romantic movie, and just relax. When you're ready to conk out and your lover still has lots of energy to spare, present him with one of the erotic videos that you wrapped and stashed last trimester. You might also hand him a bottle of massage oil. He'll know how to take it from there and you'll have sweet dreams.

10. Pelvic Pains and Pressures

When your baby moves down into your pelvis, you may experience sharp pains in the middle of your pelvic bone or at the bottom of your spine. You may even feel a prickling sensation in your cervix, the way your arm or leg feels after it has "fallen asleep" and is "waking up."

These stabbing pains sometimes come with no warning, but since they're often triggered by certain movements, you can try to avoid them.

For example, lifting up your legs to get out of bed or to put on your socks can send a shooting pain through your pelvic area. It's not unusual for these pains to shoot down your legs or zoom around to your lower back. Notice what movements bring on the pain, and then find a different way to accomplish your objective. If lifting your legs to put your socks or shoes on triggers this pain, try putting them on while sitting on the bed or couch with your feet at the same level as your hips. A little experimenting can go a long way now. Just take it slow and take yourself through a gentle range of movements. If you start to feel a twinge (often the precursor to these pains) stop what you're doing, slowly reverse the movement you were making, and try a different angle or direction.

Of course, whatever you discover about how to avoid these stabbing pains will be of supreme importance when you're making love. Fortunately, many women are very comfortable lying on their left side with their belly and their right leg propped up on pillows. Enjoying a little slow, rhythmic intercourse in this position can actually provide relief from the painful sensations brought on by walking and other "upwardly mobile" movements.

CHART 6.1   WHAT'S GOING ON INSIDE?

Third Trimester

MONTH SEVEN

- During the seventh month, your baby gains at least 1 pound and you gain between 3 and 5 pounds. Your baby's arms and legs are stronger and longer, so you may feel more vigorous movements, including kicking and punching.
- Early this month, a significant development occurs to prepare your baby to breathe outside of the womb. Cells lining the rapidly developing air sacs in the baby's lungs (alveoli) begin to secrete a soapy substance called "surfactant." This substance prevents the new air sacs from collapsing.
- Your baby's eyelids open during the seventh month and he or she can see, hear, smell, and taste. At this stage, your little one can respond to touch and sound from outside the womb.

MONTH EIGHT

- This month your baby's brain will grow rapidly and he or she will experience definite REM and non-REM sleep stages. (Dreaming occurs during the REM sleep stage.) Your baby can also blink its eyes in reaction to outside light.
- Most of your baby's growth from this point on will be in weight, rather than length. The baby's fat deposits double, smoothing out some of the wrinkles and creating a softer, more rounded appearance. This extra fat will help your baby's body regulate its temperature after birth.

[Continued on next page]

- Your baby will probably have hiccups from time to time, which will feel like sudden jerks. These are normal and don't hurt you or the baby.
- Up until the seventh month or so, babies usually lie in the womb in the breech position, because the pear-shaped uterus makes this the most roomy and comfortable position. Most babies will turn to the head-down position by the thirty-fourth week of pregnancy.
- By the end of this month, baby weighs 3 to 4 pounds and is 16 to 18 inches long.

MONTH NINE

- During the final month in the womb, your baby gains a good deal of fat, apparently in preparation for his or her entry into the world.
- As your baby runs out of room in your uterus, he or she spends most of the time tucked up like a little ball, but you will still be able to feel movements.
- Your baby breathes, blinks, sucks its thumb, opens and closes its hands, turns its head, and seems to be testing out and practicing the motor skills he or she will need after birth.
- By the time you deliver, your baby will probably weigh between 6 and 8 pounds and measure 19 to 21 inches.

Tips and Techniques for the Third Trimester

Let's face it, no matter how much you normally enjoy sex, it's just not going to be at the top of your list right now. Even so, commit to making time and saving energy for lovemaking at least twice a month if at all possible. You both need the tension and stress release right now, and you'll both benefit by the intimate connection. It's also a way to reassure each other that you can be parents and still be lovers. This is an important mind-set to reinforce in the weeks and months before your little one enters the scene.

Many couples shift the emphasis of their sex play from intercourse to cuddling, massaging, mutual masturbation, and oral sex during the last month or so. One of the big bonuses is that you now have new incentive to explore alternate ways of giving each other pleasure. Some couples have stated that they were getting into a sexual rut until they hit the eighth month of pregnancy—at which point they began trying things they'd never even thought of before! So, keep an open mind and you never know what might develop.

For most women, intimacy, bonding, and a sense of security are more important than great orgasms right now. So, although there will be innovations happening in your sex life (necessity is the mother of invention) make sure you also plan some intimate activities that are not sexual in nature. This is the time to do all the stuff that people say they like to do in personal ads. You can almost hear the soft music in the background when you envision walking hand-in-hand with your lover by the light of the moon. Seriously though, taking a moonlit walk can be incredibly romantic (provided you live in a safe area). While you're out there, pick out a star and make a wish together.

An old-fashioned form of intimacy that very few couples practice today is reading love poetry to each other. In the seventeenth century, reading poetry to a woman was as intimate as getting to second or third base in the twenty-first century. Even though you may think this sounds really corny, give it a try. You can each pick just one poem to read to each other. You'll probably be surprised how much you actually like this. If you're less of a romantic and you feel very silly reading a love poem, or being read to, then you may end up giggling or laughing, which is just as good!

One of my personal intimacy favorites is something that a friend of mine started a month before she gave birth, and still does now—eight years later! One day when Anne was in the grocery store stocking up on diapers and other last-minute baby items, she decided to buy a few packages of alphabet magnets. She had a fond flashback to her own childhood and how much she loved playing with the colorful letter magnets on the big white refrigerator. Although she bought them for the baby, when she got home, she started playing with them and ended up making a "sign" for her husband, Lee. It was a simple message: "Lee, I love loving you. Anne." When Lee came home and opened the refrigerator, he did a double take and then broke into a wide grin. Although it was a simple gesture, and Anne had said those words to him many times, Lee said that seeing it in color on the refrigerator door somehow made it more official. From that day on, Anne and Lee took turns "writing" each other notes in magnets on the refrigerator. It's not a daily obligation, and they don't have assigned weeks to change the message or anything complicated. They just keep all the letters up on the side of the fridge and when one of them feels inspired to write a message, they do. I called Anne today to see what the current message says. "Celebrate love." Great idea!

For Him

Now's the time to begin learning how to balance being a lover with being a caregiver. Your partner needs you to be attentive and affectionate with her and she also needs you to be extremely understanding. This can be pretty hard to do if you're feeling like you're the last thing on her mind. A lot of men complain that their wives demote them from the equal role of "partner" to the position of "servant" and expect them to understand and be cheerful about it. If your wife behaves like this, try to gently point out that you are willing to do whatever she needs, but that you are doing it as her partner in love and partner in having the baby together. Tell her that it's important to you that she continues to see you as her lover and her hero—not just the guy who's supposed to do everything that she can't or shouldn't do when she's eight months' pregnant.

With that said, the more you help her and take care of her, the more energy she will have when she goes into labor to deliver your baby. Everything you give to your partner will come back to you tenfold. Women whose mates stand by them during this time are eternally grateful and happy to show it.

Now, as far as sex goes, like it or not, it's going to be her call until the baby is born and for a while afterward, too. The gallant and valiant thing to do is to lovingly honor her wishes. If you could really imagine what it's like to be eight or nine months' pregnant, it would be easy for you to take the high road and be completely understanding and compassionate even when you're hornier than hell and your wife would rather walk across a bed of hot coals than have sex. I don't want to mislead you, though. While most women don't consider having sex a very high priority, especially after the eighth month, there will probably be times when she will be feeling aroused and want to be satisfied.

A yummy sex treat for your wife at this time is a deluxe hot oil treatment. Make sure the bedroom is a comfortable temperature, cover the bed with a few bath sheets, and provide at least six pillows. Heat up some almond or olive oil, so that it's warmer than skin temperature, but not so warm that it feels uncomfortable or hot. Tell your lover that you have a special treat for her, and that you expect nothing in return. (I suggest you tell her what you're planning ahead of time so she can choose the day and time.) Let her know that you just want to please her and make her feel wonderful, and then massage her to sleep. (By the way, if the word "hero" doesn't normally make it to your wife's list of adjectives to describe you—it will after this.)

Help your lover lie down on the bed on her left side. She will probably want to put a pillow or two under her head, a couple to support her belly, and another two or three to elevate her right leg. Begin by gently massaging the top and back of her head, her forehead, temples, cheeks, and chin. Now, put some of the heated oil on your hands and begin to massage her neck, shoulders, arms, and hands. Massage her back, starting with the nape of her neck and working your way down to her buttocks, legs, and feet. Gently rub oil around her breasts (avoid her nipples), her belly, between her thighs, and finally her vagina. Your objective is to help her float away to the land of nirvana while you give her the most teasingly tender oral sex that you have ever given her. Make it slow and sexy, all the while telling her how much she turns you on. After she's had one or several orgasms, give her a gentle rubdown or back scratch, cover her up, fluff her pillows, and kiss her good night. By the way, remember when you get into the heat of things that you promised you didn't want anything in return. If you try to mount her now, your rating as a compassionate lover will definitely slide. If you don't think you will be able to hold yourself back sexually, masturbate before you begin the massage.

Aside from helping your wife, and giving her great orgasms when she's up for them, there are lots of other intimate things you can do for her and with her. Some women love it when their husband washes their hair, or shaves their legs—which are now increasingly more difficult to see and reach. If your lover likes to keep her nails polished, offer to paint her toenails. Seriously. A few years back a magazine ad portrayed a shirtless sexy guy painting his lover's toenails. Women went gaga over this! I heard a group of middle-aged women lamenting over the fact that their husbands would never do that for them. When one of the women said her husband had done it for her, her comment was received with a mixture of wistful expressions and more than a few daggers. Oddly enough, the idea of our mate painting our toenails seems to trigger some sort of primitive female lust response. You may not see the results of your good deed right away, but bide your time. I guarantee you that at some point your wife is going to be bragging to her girlfriends that when she was pregnant her hubby polished her toenails! This memory is sure to make her smile and give her libido a rev every time she thinks of it.

For Her

More than a few women admit that they didn't learn how to perform good oral sex until their final months of pregnancy. It's not that these women had never pleased their lovers orally before, it's just that people tend to think of oral sex as "foreplay" instead of a very satisfying sexual event in itself—which is what it actually is. A woman who wants to be rated as an awesome lover simply must perfect the fine art of fellatio. You'll get some of the finer details on this valuable skill in Chapter Seven, but for now, just know that giving oral sex is one of the things that men say their wives either don't do often enough, or don't do very well. Something that may surprise you is that most men do want a woman to swallow their semen, no matter what the politically correct answer for this question is these days.

I can't speak for every man, but I'd have to say in most cases a man likes it when his partner swallows. A lot of men also "get off" by ejaculating on their lover's breasts or belly, but your willingness to swallow says something on a deeper, more primal level. If your pregnancy hormones have made the taste objectionable or downright gagging, by all means skip it! However, if it just tastes a little odd, try sliding his penis just slightly back farther into your mouth just as he's climaxing. That way the semen misses most of the taste buds on your tongue and goes down your throat. A refreshing sip of lemon water makes the perfect chaser for a shot of semen.

Some couples have concerns about semen being potentially harmful to the developing baby. This isn't surprising, considering that as recently as 1976, some doctors and other experts were still telling women not to swallow semen in the eighth or ninth month of pregnancy because it could induce premature labor. Your husband's ejaculate is nothing more than an organic mixture, made mostly of spermatozoa (sperm cells that look like tadpoles under a microscope), protein, and sugar. If you've heard old wives' tales that claim that ejaculate contains a mysterious substance that, if swallowed, can make the baby want to suddenly burst into the world, relax.

Not so long ago, people believed that the womb was a part of the stomach, or in some way connected, so that whatever a woman swallowed eventually made its way to the uterus. In medieval times, people believed that there was a direct line between the mouth and the vagina, with the womb between the two. If a woman wanted to know if she was pregnant, she went to bed with a clove of garlic in her vagina. If her breath did not smell like garlic the following morning, it was because the baby was blocking the odor, stopping it from rising up to the mouth. While it's true that your baby ingests part of whatever you eat or drink, a few teaspoons of semen is the equivalent of a mouthful of a protein shake, so far as the impact on the baby is concerned. So, there's no risk whatsoever.

Whether you're on the receiving end of some great oral sex, or you're watching TV in bed or reading, pillows are your new best friends right now. Any woman who's ever had a baby will know what I mean, and the rest of you are about to find out. Every pillow in the house ends up on the bed. Essential for propping and cushioning yourself while sleeping, pillows can also make the difference between sex that is awkward and cumbersome and sex that is actually quite heavenly. Now's the time to splurge on pillows of various shapes and sizes. When you have everything positioned "just so," making love and lounging can be an awesome way to spend a Sunday afternoon.

As your motherhood blooms ever larger, you may find yourself slipping into the "mommy mode" and feeling less like your husband's lover. Some of this is hormonal, but regardless of what's triggering it, make it a habit of questioning new rules that you think you or your husband should adopt, sexually or otherwise. On the days when the nurturing instincts are high and you feel like baking cookies or folding the baby blankets in the nursery one more time, just enjoy it and go with the flow. But if you suddenly start feeling like having wild sex, head for the nearest lingerie or adult sex shop and pick up the naughtiest outfit or accessory that you can find and remind yourself that even Mommy can be very hot and horny!

The next chapter discloses some of the sexiest secrets to four-star foreplay and sex without penetration. You will also discover how you and your partner can stay intimately connected outside of your bedroom.

Chapter Seven

Lovemaking Without Penetration
and Intimacy Alternatives

Although most women can have sex throughout a pregnancy, some serious conditions require abstaining from intercourse, and sometimes even forgoing orgasms. Although it sounds like bad news, this sort of experience can actually bring couples much closer together and result in even greater intimacy and passion in the long run. Meanwhile, although this chapter is *dedicated* to those couples who are experiencing high-risk pregnancies, it is *written* for everyone.

Every couple can fortify the foundation of their love affair by expanding their sexual repertoire. Intercourse is just one of many pleasing sexual possibilities. Remember how exciting giving or getting a "hand job" used to be—before you started having intercourse? It can still be that exciting, only better, because now you know more about how to please your partner and yourself. Mastering the art of oral sex is another fantastic way to make your sex life more exciting and fulfilling. This chapter offers important tips for those people who are still "in the dark" about this alternative path to orgasm.

Meanwhile, all couples can also benefit by learning how to be intimate without being sexual. Whether you're one of the couples who is abstaining from sex or you're not, this chapter is an opportunity to explore new realms of closeness and deepen your friendship, loyalty, and understanding.

If you doctor tells you that you must abstain from sex, be sure to ask for a clear explanation of your condition and specific "cans" and "can'ts." Ask your physician if abstaining from sex means no intercourse, no orgasms, or both? It's important to get this clarified because a lot of women who are told not to have intercourse can still have orgasms with no risk to the baby. Each woman and each pregnancy is different, so it is very important to be under the care of a physician whose advice you can trust and follow.

Some of the conditions that prevent a woman from having an active sex life during pregnancy include placenta previa, placenta abruption, a prematurely thinning cervix, a previous miscarriage, abnormal bleeding, high blood pressure, and preeclampsia. If your doctor diagnoses any of these conditions, learn as much as you can about your situation so you know what's safe and what's not.

Sex Without Penetration

If intercourse is off-limits, but you're still allowed to have orgasms, I highly recommend mastering the art of using your hands and your mouth to pleasure each other. I also encourage couples to practice mutual masturbation, which can be an incredible turn-on, once you get past your initial inhibitions. The following three sections will give you all the information you need to begin perfecting and polishing your skills!

Oral Sex Tips for Her

I think the biggest mistake women make when they perform oral sex on a man is that they're too rough. It's ironic, because "being too rough" is many women's number one complaint about the way men *give* oral sex.

Think about it in the reverse. When your mate performs oral sex on you, do you want him to take his tongue and rub it really hard on your clitoris, back and forth? Or do you want to feel his soft tongue and lips all over, not just on your clitoris. And it feels good when it's soft and you can feel his lips and the tongue. So think about that because that's what men like too.

When you give your partner "head," the goal is to create pleasing and unique sensations with your tongue, mouth, and hands. Don't think of your mouth as a "stand-in" for your vagina, because despite what you've seen in porn movies, thrusting his penis in and out of your mouth isn't the most desirable approach.

Most of the men that I've interviewed say that women need to use their lips and tongue more. They want to feel your lips and tongue teasing and flickering around the head of their penis while you work your hand on the shaft and the testicles.

Keep your lips and your tongue very soft and lax, and just tease and massage the head of the penis with your mouth, lips, and tongue as much as you can. Keep your tongue and lips very soft, while at the same time massaging the shaft of the penis and gently fondling his testicles.

Another technique that feels really good for a man involves keeping his testicles from retreating back up into his body when he starts to get aroused. Gently take his balls in your hand, and using your thumb and first finger, make a loose ring around the top of his scrotum. Then, give it a gentle little tug, in essence, pulling his balls farther away from his body. (Remember that you're not squeezing, just gently pulling.) Meanwhile, continue teasing the head of his penis with your lips and your tongue very softly.

An alternate version of this "ring" technique is to add an extra finger or two into the mix. While you're forming the ring with your thumb and forefinger, use one of your other fingers to softly stroke the area behind the testicles—the ultimate pleasure for a guy. They love that. And a few of them like it if that finger ventures back a little farther into the nether regions. Keep in mind that if your mate likes his anus involved during oral sex, the goal is probably not to actually stick your finger inside the anus. Most men just want you to apply pressure to the exterior by massaging a circle around the anal opening. Some men want you to stick a finger in there but most of them just want it massaged with a good deal of pressure.

If you're concerned about scraping your partner's penis with your teeth, invest in some "head candy." It's a gummy type of candy that you can put over your teeth while you give head. It comes in different flavors and slowly dissolves in your mouth. But, actually, it's not necessary to open your mouth so wide that you risk hurting the penis with your teeth. Most men aren't looking for you to perform a "deep throat"! What most of them really want is to feel some pressure up and down the shaft of the penis, while your lips and your tongue kiss and caress the head of his penis. It really doesn't matter if the pressure on the shaft is from your mouth or your hands, so there's no need to risk scraping him with your teeth, or gagging yourself.

The most sensitive parts of the penis are around the rim of the head and on the little crease underneath the head, called the "frenulum." Flicking your tongue back and forth across the frenulum, licking it from top to bottom, and swirling your tongue around the head of the penis, while it's in your mouth, all are sure-fire penis pleasers!

Also, although soft lips are often the way to go, just for variety, mix it up from time to time. One way to add some spice is to purse your lips, making a tight seal. Then, while holding his penis in your hand, push it up against your lips, and then force it into your mouth, so that it makes a little "pop" sound. You only push the head in, and then you soften your lips, pull his penis back out of your mouth, and repeat the process a few times.

The main thing to remember is that the best "blow jobs" are not hard and fast. They're soft, teasing, and sensual. If you can just think of it as if you are french-kissing his penis, you'll be giving him exactly what he wants.

Also, it's perfectly okay to swallow semen when you're pregnant. It won't hurt you or the baby, and in fact will give you a bit of extra protein.

Oral Sex Tips for Him

Unfortunately, most men don't know the first thing about how to properly perform oral sex on a woman. There is a prevailing myth that the only sensitive part of a woman's anatomy is the clitoris. In all fairness to men, I have to add that some women (in their hurry to climax) repeatedly direct men right to this hot spot, which helps to spread the prevailing myth!

The truth about a woman's most sensitive spots is so well hidden because many women don't even know how many they have or where they're all located. So, here's a brief tour. Obviously, the clitoris is sensitive and can be the starting point of many a great orgasm. However, stimulating the area right around the clitoris and the internal and external labia can be just as arousing, if not more so.

Another part of a woman's body that is extremely sensitive is her frenulum. The frenulum is the spot before the clitoris where the internal labia meet. It forms that nice little "V," where the labia starts to branch out from the body. It's between the clitoris and urethral opening.

Right below the frenulum is a U-shaped area of soft tissue called spongiosum. Spongiosum is a very soft, spongy tissue and it's also what the "G" spot is made of. The "G" spot is actually an exposed area of spongiosum tissue inside the vagina. The "U" spot is the only spot on a woman's body where the spongiosum is exposed to the air. The U spot is immediately below the frenulum and above the urethral opening. That U-shaped area is very sensitive. I suggest giving it some gentle attention with your lips and tongue, but don't use your fingers here, because it's way too sensitive for that. By flicking the tip of your tongue and softly licking this "U," while avoiding the clitoris, you can create a very different and exciting sensation.

Another area that is highly sensitive is the "taint." It's the area between the vagina and the anus. I call it the "taint" because it ain't the ass and it ain't the pussy. Tickling or stroking this area with the flat part of a finger, while you caress her vagina, inside and out, with your mouth and tongue, is guaranteed to produce satisfaction!

Pay attention to the entire vagina and surrounding area, as well as her breasts, lips, neck, and so on.

Red Flag

The one thing that you should *never* do, *especially during pregnancy,* is blow air into the vagina. Some couples have a fetish for this, but it can cause an air embolism, which is basically a pocket of air in the blood stream that can work its way into the arteries, possibly reaching your heart or brain and causing serious, permanent damage or worse.

Changing Tastes

Some men say that their partners have a different scent and taste when they are pregnant. It's not a matter of "better or worse," it's just different. This happens because of the pregnancy hormones and the changes in your partner's body chemistry. It doesn't mean that she isn't clean, or that something is wrong. Most men say that they notice a difference, but that it's not objectionable, and some men say the new scent or taste really turns them on.

If you're put off by the changes, try using some "head candy" (gummy candy that fits over your teeth and slowly dissolves) or try out some chocolate body paints with a little whipped cream on top.

Masturbation

Masturbation is not only safe during pregnancy, it's highly recommended, especially when you do it with your partner.

This can be a really exciting part of sex play for all couples, but for those who are unable to have intercourse together, mutual masturbation is a wonderful way to stay sexually connected. Whether you're doing it to each other, or watching each other do it to yourselves, it will definitely help you to maintain the image of each other as lovers and sexual creatures.

You shouldn't insert dildos or other devices into the vagina when you're pregnant, but it is safe to use a vibrator externally. And by the way, for those women who have never used a vibrator, that's a crying shame! This is definitely the time to try it. I practically wore mine out during my pregnancies.

It's also safe for a woman's partner to insert his fingers into her vagina, as long as his hands are clean and his fingernails are filed to a smooth finish. Because a woman's pH balance is different during pregnancy, she is very susceptible to various types of vaginal infections, so cleanliness is a must during this time.

If you feel inhibited about the idea of masturbating in front of each other, do it in the dark the first couple of times. Start out by feeling each other in the dark, and then you can work your way up to soft candlelight or brighter if you like.

Even if you think this would be over the top for you and your partner, commit to giving it a chance. Beginning in the dark really does work. It's kind of naughty, and you don't have to see it with your eyes. You can see it with your fingertips. He can feel you touching yourself in the dark and vice versa. Not only is it incredibly erotic, but you also learn more about what each other likes.

When I was pregnant, when I didn't feel like having intercourse, we often had mutual masturbation. I would masturbate myself and he would watch while he masturbated himself, or we would touch each other at the same time, both of which I found to be incredibly arousing. Many women discover that they sometimes prefer this type of sex play over intercourse because it adds a different dimension of intimacy to their love affair. As every sexually experienced woman knows, intercourse isn't all it's about for us, despite what most men may think or wish to believe.

A great activity that can be used as an arousal technique leading to mutual masturbation or oral sex is the "pregnant centerfold." This fun and intimate "photo shoot" encourages couples to immortalize the woman at her pregnant best through photos that the man takes of his woman wearing sexy lingerie and posing in her most erotic positions.

Now's the time to get creative and come up with some sexy innovations of your own!

Intimacy Alternatives

First of all, whether you're one of the women who shouldn't orgasm during pregnancy or not, you and your partner will benefit by reading this section of the chapter. One of the elements that couples tend to lose over time is the sense of sexual urgency they felt for each other when they first met. When was the last time you wanted each other so desperately that you had to do it in the car before you drove home? If you're like most couples, it's been a while. Maybe a long while, and probably way too long if you really think about it.

One way to rekindle this yearning is through abstinence. When you want to have sex with each other, but you can't or don't, the embers of desire tend to keep smoldering for a long time. This is particularly true if you continue to connect in intimate ways that fan the flames of passion, but stop short of igniting a full blown fire. This can be a tricky line to walk, particularly for the woman. The last thing you want right now is to get really turned on and not be able to bring the passion to a climax. So, it's really up to you to call the shots concerning what you want to do or don't want to do.

If your partner is having a difficult time understanding or empathizing with the depth of your condition, explain it to him by saying something like this: "What if I handcuffed you to the bed, played with you until you had a huge hard-on, and then walked away? Well that's what it feels like for me to get really aroused and not be able to do anything about it. It might be a pleasant form of torture if it only lasted a few minutes, but under the circumstances I really need to be able to draw the line and have you respect that." Some women swear that actions work better than words in this scenario, but I'll leave that decision entirely up to you.

Massage

One of the most intimate ways for couples to connect is by giving each other the gift of massages. This gift is worth the price of gold to any woman who is in her second or third trimester of pregnancy because she is most likely experiencing discomfort and pain in various areas of her body, particularly her lower back, feet, and calves.

For Him

The massage should be relaxing and done to relieve discomfort and pain. The key is to completely avoid all of the sexual areas, so your partner can relax and focus on releasing stress and tension. She should not feel like you are buttering her up in exchange for oral sex. She should be able to completely get into the massage and feel comforted knowing that you have no expectations.

A really good massage position is for your partner to lie on her left side with a pillow under her belly and another one between her knees. Use a natural oil such as olive or almond and begin by massaging her neck and shoulders, and then work your way down her back. Give special attention to the area around her shoulder blades and to her lower back and sides. You can also massage her tummy, which is very safe as long as you don't apply a lot of pressure. Then move down and knead and massage her buttocks and the fronts and backs of her legs. Finish by massaging her feet, kissing her, and tucking her comfortably under the blankets to rest quietly.

For Her

Of course, you are wise to repay the favor when you feel up to it. Even a five-minute neck and shoulder massage can let your partner know how much you appreciate him and want him to feel good. When you have extra energy, you can surprise him by ending the massage with a blow job or by masturbating him with your hands. But remember that the massage is your primary purpose for practicing intimacy alternatives.

The Not So Dirty Dozen

1.   Love Connection

I shared the "Love Connection" exercise with you in Chapter Five and suggested that you and your partner practice it each day. In the event that you haven't adopted it as a daily practice, let me refresh your memory on how it's done.

For thirty seconds, twice a day, sit or stand face-to-face with your partner, hold hands, and look into each other's eyes. Silently communicate the love and gratitude you feel for each other, and then share a heart-to-heart hug.

Many of the couples in high-risk pregnancies like to do this practice in bed each night before they go to sleep. They lie facing each other and they each put one hand on "the baby" and hold hands with the other. Couples said that their babies frequently kicked or moved when they connected like this. There are lots of different ways that you can practice the Love Connection, and I encourage you to be creative and have fun with this.

If you feel awkward at first, or think this is silly, or one of you wants to do it and the other doesn't, just be willing to try it for seven days. Some couples laugh and giggle when they first start doing this. That's great! It doesn't have to be some big, heavy, solemn moment. The idea is just to connect and feel each other's love. It will be a little different each time.

2.   Pillow Talk

There's so little "pillow talk" going on in bedrooms nowadays that the term itself is starting to become antiquated. For the "youngsters" in the crowd, pillow talk is when you cuddle up next to each other in bed and you share your hopes, dreams, gratitude, and love. It's not a long, drawn-out conversation. It's more like speaking in headlines. The idea is just to spend a few minutes each morning or evening, sharing your minds and hearts with each other.

Following are a few guidelines:

- Be present in the moment.
- Speak from your heart.
- Listen with your heart.
- Do not ask any questions.
- Do not ask any favors.
- Do not express disapproval in any form—for your mate or about yourself. (That sort of conversation is what I call "table talk," and should never happen in your bedroom!)

Once pillow talk becomes part of your daily bonding, it will be very spontaneous and will simply flow for a moment or two without either of you consciously thinking about the guidelines or what you want to say.

But for now, the following are some ideas can help to get you started. Remember that pillow talk is completely "positive." If there's an area that you can't say something good about, then you don't say anything about it at all.

"I love it when you—"
"I'm so proud of you for—"
"I appreciate you because—"
"When you smile at me, I—"

"If I knew I couldn't fail, I would—"

3.   Sunday Driving

You can do this any day of the week, but the couple who shared it with me did it as a Sunday ritual. On the first Sunday of every month, they would buy a newspaper, and pick up a picnic lunch from the nearby deli. Armed with excellent road maps (and a cell phone, just in case), they picked a general direction and drove for thirty minutes or so, until they found a place they wanted to stop. After relaxing, reading the paper, and enjoying their lunch, they would begin their adventure of finding their way back home.

This sort of thing obviously shouldn't be done if you're surrounded by unsafe neighborhoods, or if you're due to deliver soon. However, seeing new roads, new shops, new views, and new pieces of the countryside is an exciting stimulus for your mind and all of your senses. Mixing relaxation with adventure is a wonderful way to de-stress, connect, and discover new things together.

A variation on this is to do it on the Internet. For example, you select a destination anywhere locally, or in the world, and then you explore it online together.

4.   Romantic Movies

A well-made romantic movie is a delightful two-hour vacation. Ask your friends and coworkers to tell you the names of their favorite romance movies of all time. Make a list and take turns picking which one you will go to see or rent. I suggest you ask some teenagers this question, too, because some of the more innocent romance films are the most heartwarming. Seek out movies with lots of intimacy, but not too much sexual contact. Avoid the dramas, lean toward the romantic comedies, and no matter what else, "happy endings" are a must!

5.   Love Songs

I can't speak for the men on this one, but just about every woman I know has a fantasy about her partner singing her a love song. This is actually a fantasy that is not so hard to fulfill, providing that your partner is willing to play along. If not, give the gift of a love song to him or her anyway, just for fun.

Even though the "karaoke craze" seems to have hit its peak, and begun to fade, there are still plenty of places in just about every city that have karaoke nights. I suggest going there, picking out a love song, and singing it to your partner. Even if you don't think you have a good voice, if you can carry a tune, the modern technology will support you and it will be fun for both of you!

If you feel nervous about singing in front of other people, doing it can be an exciting rush. Plus, the worse case scenario is that you end up providing some much-needed comic relief to your lives. If even the thought of doing this mortifies you, then consider renting a karaoke machine and serenading your lover in the privacy of your own home.

Of course, if you're comfortable with your voice, or you happen to be a singer or a musician, you can do this without the aid of karaoke!

6.   Shaping Up

Working out together, whether it's walking around the block, playing tennis, or attending a yoga class, can bring couples closer together. There's something about sharing a common experience in which you're both exerting an effort and doing something that's good for yourself that fosters the feeling of being on the same team. This is particularly helpful and important during a high-risk pregnancy, when worries and fears can sometimes make you feel at odds with each other, even though you're both on the same side.

Strengthening your connection by toning and strengthening your body is most certainly a win-win for both of you, as well as for your baby. Exercise also releases stress and creates feel-good hormones that may also have a pleasing effect on your baby. Participating in some sort of exercise or sport with your partner on a regular basis also provides the perfect forum to give each other support, encouragement, and praise. Plus, people who exercise tend to sleep more soundly and every pregnant couple can benefit by this one!

7.   Holding Hands

Creating deeper intimacy doesn't have to be complicated or choreographed. Often, all it takes is getting back to basics. Holding hands is a perfect example of connecting with each other on a very intimate, yet nonsexual level. You can say volumes with the squeeze of your hand or the soft caress of your thumb. This simple practice also reinforces your role as lovers and friends. It's symbolic of your bond with each other and creates a sense of comfort and reassurance.

Holding hands is also playful and lighthearted. If you've stopped holding hands, it's time to re-initiate this connection. If your partner is not comfortable with public displays of affection, then hold hands while you're at home together sitting on the sofa, or reach across the table and hold one of his hands for a moment during dinner.

8.   Candlelight Dinners

You don't have to spend a lot of money to enjoy a candlelight dinner together. In fact, one of my girlfriends used to serve fast food on her special china with candles and flowers on the table and the whole deal! It's not how fancy the food or the dishes are, though, it's the idea that you love each other enough to light a few candles and turn an ordinary meal into something a little more special.

If your budget permits, by all means go out a treat yourself to a great candlelight meal from time to time. It's a nice break in the routine and gets you out of your environment with all of its built-in distractions. When you sit in a restaurant, for that hour or two, leave your "to-do" list and your troubles behind you. Celebrate yourselves, each other, and the love you share.

9.   Sharing a Sunset

When was the last time you and your partner shared the beauty of a sunset together?

This is another one of those very basic and simple ways for a couple to connect on a deeper level. As you watch the colors in the sky changing as the sun slips over the horizon, you can't help but feel a sense of wonder. The magic is that you experience this beauty together. Without saying a single word, you both simultaneously experience a moment of awe. It's really incredible if you can actually be out in nature for your sunset together, but the view from the top of a city skyscraper can be magnificent, too.

If you're really into sharing sunsets, here's another idea. Once a month, throughout the pregnancy, go somewhere picturesque to watch the sunset and bring a camera with a tripod. Then take a photo of the two of you kissing with the colors of the sunset in the background, making sure to position yourself so that your belly is in view! This set of photos will make a wonderful chronicle of the pregnancy and be a celebration of the lovers that you continue to be. This is also the perfect time to make a Love Connection! (See number one in this list.)

10.   Snuggle Bunnies

This one is a popular favorite for men and women! Put on your softest, most comfortable nightgown, sweat suit, or pajamas, curl up under a blanket together, and simply snuggle up. You can do this in front of a fire, while you're listening to music, or even when you're watching television.

Just an hour or so of "snuggle bunny" will make you both feel warm, secure, and connected. (If you live in a hot climate you'll probably want to wear soft, flowing clothes, and may want to forgo the blanket, or replace it with a light sheet.)

Some couple really love doing this together and make it even more playful by rubbing noses, wriggling around together under the blanket, or using pet names with each other. Other couples simply like the comfortable togetherness.

11.   Laughing Together

There's no longer any doubt that laughter is good medicine for the body, mind, and soul! The physical act of laughing has been proven to significantly reduce stress, tension, and high blood pressure. There's even evidence that laughing decreases our chances of getting heart disease and certain forms of cancer. While it doesn't create actual endorphins (feel-good hormones), it does produce an endorphin-like effect.

Aside from the physical perks, laughing together is fun and creates warm memories. When I ask couples to recall the most memorable moments in their courtship or marriage, the moments of laughter almost always outnumber the others. So go to a comedy club, rent some funny movies, tell each other jokes, and share the amusing stories and anecdotes that you hear at work or through the media with each other.

12.   Counting Your Blessings

There are few things in life that remind us more clearly of our good fortune as counting our blessings. Reflecting on all of the aspects of your relationship and pregnancy for which you are grateful will help you to keep your hearts open to each other, which is the most powerful connection of all.

Every now and again, set aside fifteen to thirty minutes to count your blessings together. The idea is to list all of the specific events, favors, behaviors, character traits, gifts, and so on that you are grateful about in yourselves, each other, the relationship, and the pregnancy.

You can do this two different ways and they're both great. You can use one sheet of paper and make the list together. Or, you can both make your own list and then give it to the other when you are finished.

Save your lists of "blessings" in a special box or envelope. When one or both of you is feeling low or discouraged, pull out your lists and read them again!

Although I've given you a dozen intimacy alternatives, don't stop there. I encourage you and your partner to come up with your own ideas because the ones you create together will likely be the most meaningful and fulfilling. Keep in mind that some of the best intimacy builders are the most simple. Holding hands, hugging, kissing, and looking into each other's eyes are basic ingredients for strengthening and maintaining your connection as lovers. From time to time, mix it up by doing something that is a little more elaborate or takes a bit more planning, just to make it more interesting.

Chapter Eight shows you how to make the decisions that will result in a sensual childbirth experience.

Chapter Eight

Sensual Birth

We have all seen so many depictions of the birth process in the media that it seems like an oxymoron to put sensual and birth in the same sentence. What can be sensual about a woman writhing in pain while birthing a basketball?

The physical sensations of childbirth might not be pleasant, but the emotional experience of sharing it with the one you love is what makes the birth process sensual and intimate. I have heard many men say that the birth of their child was the happiest moment of their lives. I really think that for some of them it outweighs getting married or even having sex for the first time. The miracle of the birth of his own offspring seems to change a man forever.

The birth of their child is one of or is the happiest moment of a man's life. However, contrary to today's popular opinion, I believe that having a man witness the nitty gritty of childbirth can be a big mistake. Men have been told to accompany their wives in the labor and delivery room if they want to have any respect as a caring husband and father. Men used to wait in the waiting room, pacing, smoking, and preparing to give out cigars. This is not great either and you would be hard pressed nowadays to find a waiting room that would let you smoke a cigar.

I don't suggest keeping husbands out of the delivery room, I just think we need to think of the ramifications of allowing a man to see his former Pleasure Central expanded, bloody, and gross. I am not trying to dismiss a man's ability to support his wife during this process, I just have spoken to enough men who feel that imprinted image has done very little to support a post-birth sex life.

Let's face it, women do not have to watch the process. We are too busy pushing to pay attention to what is going on in our nether regions. Even if there is a mirror strategically placed to provide a front-row view, we are in no state of mind to interpret an upside-down image of our innards.

But a man standing ready to catch the baby as it slides into this world has to watch everything. I think that if a man has the stomach for blood he would enter the medical field. Not all men can deal with it. I think we should protect their delicate visual brains from a picture imprint that could *affect* their arousal potential for a long time.

If you both really want the father to be present in the delivery room and he plans to see everything, that is a very personal choice. But educate yourselves. The more you know and understand the less it will have a negative impact on your sex life and relationship.

I believe in intimacy and comfort between people but I do suggest limits. When you make love, anything that gives each of you pleasure and that is agreed upon is great (but I don't suggest that couples observe each other's intimate bathroom habits). There has to be some mystery. So don't assume that "everything goes." When considering the experience you want to share during childbirth, make sure you communicate clearly what is good for you both.

A man can be in the delivery room and stand behind the drapes at the moment of truth. Turning away works too or standing close to his wife's head rather than at the point of exit. This way the parents both get to see the new baby at the same time. This is intimate without giving anyone anxiety. Although you may not agree, many men say that they have a hard time viewing the vagina as Pleasure Central after seeing all that blood and gore. They can't distinguish between what is natural, like the delivery of the placenta, and something totally yuck. It all looks the same. So if you really want to experience the birth of your child together, you might want to consider how much is too much. There may be ways to have the husband participate without having a bird's eye view.

Another reason not to have your husband watch everything is what may be some minor unpleasantries that are going to be happening to you during childbirth. Having a baby is a miracle and it is wonderful, but while giving birth you may develop hemorrhoids, and you may need an episiotomy, which elicits the same reaction in women as talking about a kick in the gonads does in men. An episiotomy is a surgical incision of the vulva to prevent tearing when the baby is pushed out. It doesn't really hurt because it is done when the baby puts pressure on the nerve endings and blocks the pain, but it is not a pretty sight. You will not necessarily be aware of it and it will happen fast, but your husband might not forget it so soon.

Women need to be somewhat sensitive to the fact that their men experience many changes that they will not readily verbalize. Men might not even be aware of them themselves. For example, although they don't readily admit it, some men have a difficult time at first being sexual with their mate when they see the baby nursing, because those breasts have been his for so long. All of sudden he realizes breasts have a biological function. After some emotional readjustment most men get over that one pretty quick. (You'll read more about this in Chapter Nine.) Women are always more in touch with their feelings. Men would sooner withdraw from their mate than admit or face what might really be going on inside.

I wanted to get this out of the way before I discuss with you how to have a sensual birth. I want you to understand my bias that intimacy and sensuality do not necessarily mean that you let everything hang out. I don't know about you, but I don't really enjoy shows that tell you the secrets behind how magicians perform their illusions. There are some things that should be left to appear like magic.

The same is true for relationships. While I advocate honesty in communication to promote intimacy, I don't think it is necessary to tell your partner everything you think or feel at every moment. Men and women are too different to expect that either species will fully enjoy the total immersion into the mind and psyche of the other. Sometimes allowing nature, chemistry, and the differences between men and women exist untouched is the best thing you can do.

Sensual birth requires support and understanding from both man and woman. It requires some imagination and the idea that the experience is special and to be savored. There are stages of labor and childbirth that need to be respected. If you know what to expect you can flow with the natural rhythms of the process and be there with each other to create an experience that is memorable beyond the obvious.

The actual process of childbirth is not as distasteful as I have made it sound. I am simply trying to help you preserve the quality of your sex life post-baby. So if what you have read so far has in any way turned you off to the process you had better get over it. At some point the baby is going to come out. You can make this a really great experience with a bit of planning and the sensual imagination you have been developing throughout the pregnancy. I am not going to ignore the undeniable fact that childbirth hurts. You have many good options for coping with the pain. Although some doctors advocate childbirth without pain intervention, this is a very personal choice. *(As I once heard comedian Joan Rivers say, "My idea of natural childbirth is wearing absolutely no makeup!")* You don't have to prove anything to anyone by skipping the methods of pain relief that are available to you. There are few situations that warrant your being completely knocked out the way they did it in the "old days," but there are many options you can discuss with your doctor so you can make an informed decision. With or without pain, the process of childbirth takes a lot of energy for both parents. Good planning and communication will help you get through it in a very positive way. For some reason babies like to be born in the middle of the night, so advance preparation will help make everything run smoothly.

The first thing you are going to do to create a sensual birth is to discuss openly how you both feel about the process itself and just how much involvement you want the husband to have in the actual delivery.

The next step in preparing for a sensual birth is to discuss and determine how and where you want the baby to be born. You have many options here and you each may have your own image of where and how it should be done. One of you may not have given it any thought. But since you are going to go through this together, you really should talk about it. If you do not make your preferences known ahead of time you may be disappointed when the time comes. Also, discussing and planning the birth leads to making it a more intimate experience.

Before the actual event you can create an atmosphere of sensuality and sacredness. If you feel up to it, you can make love as much as you like. If there is no medical reason to avoid it you can take advantage of this time to have as many orgasms as you can work into your schedules.

If you are at risk for premature birth or if your water has broken (the membrane sack that surrounds your baby in the womb breaks in preparation of the beginning of labor), you should abstain. A lot of women, however, don't have their water broken until they are in the labor or birthing room. But if your water breaks prematurely (and of course it usually decides to break in public so don't even worry about it), you should not have intercourse. Without the membranes to protect it the baby could be at risk of infection.

A word about water breaking. Yes, it looks like you have peed. But think of it this way. You obviously look pregnant if you are far enough along to have your water break. So if a bystander thinks for a minute that you have peed, he or she should be put in prison for felonious stupidity. The least of your concerns should be what people think. When you are pregnant and ready to give birth, if people do not treat you like a queen, act like one anyway.

If there are no special circumstances, there is no reason why you can't have sex up until the very moment you go into labor. Making love won't prematurely induce your labor, but it can help it to start if the time is right and you are ready.

Orgasm does not bring about labor, but if labor is about to start or if you're in the very beginning stages it can facilitate the labor and make it much easier and smoother. I strongly recommend that you make love as often as you can. Talking is great and will bring you close, but sex is even better.

A few other situations warrant abstinence from sex right before delivery. If you have any risk for a premature delivery or you are carrying more than one baby, you may be advised by your doctor to avoid intercourse. There are other conditions, such as a problem with the placenta, that would indicate that intercourse should be avoided. Your doctor will tell you if such a situation exists.

If you have any unexplained bleeding you should not have intercourse but rather should contact your doctor. There may be a simple explanation, but you do not want to take any chances. Find out if there is any reason to avoid orgasm. Of course there is never any reason for a man to avoid orgasm that I know of, so exchange a luxurious massage and foot rub for some strategic rubbing that should put a smile on his face.

In the last month before delivery you might want to use a condom to avoid causing irritation while the woman's cervix is dilating. But not all physicians think this is necessary.

If the mother-to-be is not in the mood for sex right before delivery it is nothing to be concerned about. Throughout the pregnancy you have been striving for sensual and emotional intimacy and have grown as a couple. Your relationship is on solid footing and you have had some sexual experiences that you can draw upon in your twilight years. It's not unreasonable for a woman who is constipated, sore, tired, and unable to get more than five bites of food past the uterus, which is now up against her ribs, to not feel sexually intimate.

This is a very good time for cuddling, loving, planning, and preparing. This is also a very good time to plan the kind of birth experience you want and to list the things over which you can exercise some control. Some couples actually create a birth plan. They choose where they want to have the baby and preregister at the hospital of their choice. If all goes well and they are not sidetracked to another hospital for any number of logistical reasons, this will save a lot of aggravation when the baby is on its way.

The main ingredient of a sensual birth is to eliminate as much stress as possible for both parents. In fact, an English physician named Grantly Dick-Read who introduced the idea of natural childbirth in 1933 claimed that women who had less fear and tension going into their labor had a much easier time of it. He began the consideration of breathing exercises as a method of easing labor pain.

Clearly, the reduction of stress and tension creates the environment for a sensual birth. If you are mentally prepared for your birth experience, you can spend the time of labor up until delivery supporting each other and sharing in your mutual miracle.

Begin by choosing your hospital and the type of birth you hope to have. Other options, such as a home birth, require a different kind of planning. Home births can be very appealing because of the freedom they afford. A home birth is a celebration of life where you can have family and friends present and can get up and walk around without so many sterile medical restrictions.

But there are obvious drawbacks to a home birth. Most doctors will not attend a home birth. You would probably need a midwife, who at present would also have difficulty finding a medical professional to be available and on call if something were to go wrong. Home births do not rely on the many monitoring systems available in hospitals. Many people who choose to give birth at home want to avoid the monitors and other forms of equipment, but there are risks involved.

Choosing a home birth is a judgment call based on how uncomplicated the birth is likely to be. If all is uneventful, it can be a wonderful experience. If a birth is very low risk and there are backup plans made, people have expressed that they would not have wanted their birth experience any other way.

A home birth with a midwife allows attention to be paid to the needs of the mother. In many ways it is less traumatic to the husband than it is in the hospital room because the environment is more natural and he has more support.

A private labor coach, called a "doula," is focused on the needs of the mother during labor, delivery, and after the birth. Although a doula is certainly suited to a home birth situation, many women hire doulas to help them during hospital births as well.

Although I hope to give you some ideas of how to have a positive, intimate birth experience, I do believe that men are not naturally inclined to understand the birth process as much as another woman is. It's a girl thing. There are ways that husbands can be loving, comforting, and supportive, but there are just some things that men can't be expected to understand.

Many marriages have been spared some of the stress of childbirth by having other women significantly assist the laboring mother. I know men who have been greatly relieved when a female family member has acted as a substitute doula. Men can get a little frazzled when they see their wives in pain. Some men stay calm, but men are so typically problem solvers that they can't always relax and go with the flow of the delivery process. I know one woman whose husband made himself a real pest by demanding more pain medicine for his wife every time she had a contraction. This was in early labor. He probably should have gotten some medicine for himself.

Problem solving doesn't always work in this situation. A calm and steady attitude is best. Good planning can create the right atmosphere but some ground rules should be laid out ahead of time. Sometimes it is best for the husband to bring things to keep himself occupied. Though the wife might want him nearby, she might not really want him to say or do anything.

One man I know bought a miniature DVD player for the occasion, and he said it was the best money he had spent. His wife agreed. He was there to support her but he was able to back off when necessary and not hover when she needed her own space. During childbirth women often need to simply go inside themselves and experience the labor in their own way. If they are allowed to do this, the experience can be extraordinary.

Many options allow you to choose the kind of birth experience you would like. If you choose to have your baby in a hospital, you can often arrange to have what is called a "birthing room." The advantage of a birthing room is that you have your labor and delivery right in the same room. Then you can sometimes stay in the same room after the baby is born while you are going through your recovery. Whether or not you stay in the room afterward, the homey atmosphere enhances the experience of giving birth in this way. Hospitals have made their childbirth options competitive with one another, so you should shop around to see who offers the best facilities. Birthing rooms are often decorated to look like a home instead of a sterile hospital environment. They typically have their own private shower and may have some room for visitors. They are much more comfortable than the old process of labor in one room, delivery in another, and recovery in yet another.

Some hospitals offer the use of a birthing chair instead of a typical hospital table. It is an actual chair that allows the laboring mother to sit in more natural positions than you can on a flat surface. (See Chapter Two for the origins of this mechanism.)

Aside from frequent lovemaking and massaging each other to heights of ecstasy, you can take the time before the baby to plan other details of your birth experience. Throughout your pregnancy you have many opportunities to attend childbirth classes together. Lamaze is a common class that is recommended by most obstetricians.

Lamaze, which was first introduced in France in 1951 by French obstetrician Fernand Lamaze, teaches many relaxation techniques that are particularly effective in the early stages of labor. Lamaze uses guided imagery and breathing for pain management. One of the biggest advantages of the Lamaze classes is that they teach you a lot about what is happening to you during the birth process. This is a great time to bond as a couple because you attend the classes as a couple. You learn together what is happening inside the mother's body and what to expect in the process of giving birth. Lamaze classes have really become childbirth education and have given couples a chance to alleviate anxiety by affording an opportunity to ask questions and express concerns. Couples also meet other couples who are at the same stages of pregnancy. This is also very soothing to a couple who may not have had exposure to other people experiencing the same types of issues.

Another method of childbirth preparation that teaches mothers to accept the pain and work through it instead of using guided imagery or breathing to avoid feeling it is Bradley childbirth. If you find a good Bradley childbirth educator, you can also learn methods of childbirth preparation that you can do as a couple. Bradley emphasizes diet and exercise in preparation for childbirth and his was the first method to encourage husbands as birth coaches. While I may not agree with all of the results for some men, Bradley made many strides in creating options for couples who want to share the experience of childbirth.

One of the things you will learn in any of your childbirth preparation classes, or will be told by your doctor or hospital, is what to pack for the big day. You definitely do want to plan ahead for this. If this is your first baby, at the first sign of labor you might get a little "wiggy." In fact, it is amazing how some couples react. As I have already alluded, sensual birth requires a sense of calm and control over those things that can be controlled. The best way to have a sense of control is to be prepared for as many eventualities as you can conceive.

Choose lots of interesting things to pack for your labor and birth experience. You will want to pack the obvious, like toiletries. A toothbrush, shampoo, and your familiar soaps or oils will be appreciated more than you know. Pack a few nursing nightgowns if you are planning to nurse.

You will want some nursing bras because you have no idea how quickly breasts fill with milk after the baby is born. Nursing pads help to alleviate feeling wet and drippy as you get used to the process of nursing.

You should pack some maternity clothes for the trip home because there is little likelihood that you will be back to pre-pregnant shape right after birth. You will feel much lighter but your body will take a bit of time to heal. You don't want to feel discouraged. Pick something that is particularly pretty—wear maternity pants and cover them with a sexy new blouse or two. Pack a second one in case you have a slight leak. It is going to take a little time for you to get used to things.

Bring some neutral infant clothing to take baby home in. Don't forget that part. You will come home with more than you came in with. That is what you will want to pack for your stay after the baby is born. You can add things like baby announcements but don't feel obligated to do anything but bask in the glow of the new life you and your husband have brought into the world together.

Pack a separate bag of things you will want during delivery. You want to be as comfortable as possible. You should pack snacks (for your husband) and things to keep him occupied so you can avoid the urge to kill him during labor. As I will explain, there are times during the process when you do not want to be touched or bothered. You may want your husband to be around you but not so close that you can cause him bodily harm.

You won't be able to eat anything and probably will not even want to think about it. But you will be thirsty. The hospital usually has popsicles available but you may want to check ahead of time and if not, bring your own. You can pack lollipops and will be able to chew on ice chips.

When you pack your hospital bag think about how to make the birth experience intimate and sensual. In the early stage of labor you can enjoy such things as listening to soft music. You may be able to walk around the hallways to move your labor along. Bring some warm and cozy socks. For some reason, women's feet get really cold during delivery. I also don't see why you can't bring some mint or papaya foot lotion and have your hubby give you a bit of a massage. There is a window of time before you go into the second stage of labor when some rubbing will be appreciated.

You could also pack a sock filled with tennis balls. This is a great makeshift back massager. While you are in labor you can rest on your left side while your husband runs the tennis balls up and down your back. This is very soothing for back labor.

If you want your birth to be a sensual and intimate experience, be completely in the moment. Make sure you have planned ahead for things like pets or work. Make sure—as best you can—that your mutual responsibilities are covered by loved ones or friends. The best thing you can do for each other is to be there with your minds completely focused on what is happening. While I recommend hubby have things like DVDs to keep him occupied, this is just during stages when the wife needs her space. In general, the couple should be completely immersed in the moment and the experience without worrying about anything outside each other and the baby that is on the way.

This kind of focus is what connection is all about. It is what you need when you are making love, when you are talking with each other, and certainly when you are having a baby. This is one time when you should completely block out the outside world. Don't worry about in-laws or extended family. Don't even have them at the hospital if you feel they will distract you from each other. I love family, but this is a very important bonding time. You wouldn't want to have a crowd with you in your bedroom during conception would you?

During the early stage of labor you can enjoy each other. The husband can learn to read the fetal monitor if one is used and can help his wife anticipate her contractions and he can lovingly help her through them.

When the contractions get stronger in the second stage of labor called "transition," the husband might want to gauge exactly how much involvement his wife wants from him. She might want him there one minute and may be cursing him the next. Husbands, I implore you, do not take this personally. Unless your wife has opted and already been given pain relief orally or through an epidural, which blocks the pain from the lower back down, she is going to be hurting. There is almost nothing that can describe labor pain. Some people say that if the memory of it didn't wear off, which it seems to do over time, no one would ever have a second child.

The early stage of labor can last for hours or days. If the contractions are irregular or mild it is too soon to go to the hospital.

You will want to pack some mindless things for you to read if you think you will want to occupy yourself other than staring into your lover's eyes. There is nothing wrong with wanting to look at a few magazines. Leave the baby books home unless they make you happy. If they will fill you with anxiety, leave them home. The nurses will show you anything you need to know to bring your baby home with you. By the time you leave the hospital you will know how to diaper your baby, swaddle her in a blanket, and all of those things that seem so impossible. You will feel inept at first, but you will catch on.

This is not yet time to completely transition into mother mode. While you are excited about your future, you don't want to forget that you are part of a couple. It is very easy for women to want to slip into "this is only my experience" mode. Remember what you both have already learned about the issues that pop up during this time of transition. You already know these things. So remember to remember each other during this process.

If you are in early labor and not yet ready to go to the hospital, make sure if you eat that you eat very lightly. You don't want to completely ignore hunger because you have no real way of knowing how long this first stage of labor will last. It is a good idea to call your doctor if you have your doubts. Typically early or what they call "false labor" is characterized by uneven intervals of contractions that stop when you move around or change position. I hate the term "false labor" because it is not descriptive and makes women feel stupid. You are not simply having gas. You are having contractions because you are getting ready to give birth. When you are having your first baby you don't know how "real" labor feels.

This stage can take a while and your actual "real" labor will start out mildly enough that your doctor might not immediately send you to the hospital. When your contractions are coming at regular intervals that keep getting closer and closer you will call your doctor and probably head to the hospital. Your contractions will be more intense and you will know that they are labor pains. You will not be able to talk easily through them and will not be able to walk.

While you are having the mild false labor you might want to use this time to spend some last sensual hours together before your life changes forever. I like the idea of soft candlelight, sexy music, and some gentle lovin'. Nothing too much. Just some cuddling and massaging and sharing. Be into each other. Love each other and create the mental soil in which your dreams may be planted.

If you think like lovers going into the process of childbirth, you will come out of it as lovers who have brought a child into the world to expand their world. This is a much different perspective than making it the woman's experience alone. Your life will change but you will still be in this together when the baby is born. Keep the focus balanced. Baby will become the center of your world for a while, but remember that you still have a special bond. You will make love again and will share a life together of many moments like this.

When a woman is in the second stage of labor she might not be very nice. She might want to grab her husband's hand during contractions but this is not a good idea. Women are very strong and could cause some damage. Definitely do not put your penis within grabbing distance. As the pain increases she might have some thoughts better left unsaid.

As I have already discussed, a husband's role at this time is to basically stay out of the way unless his wife requests his presence. He is to completely subjugate his ego and his need not to be sworn at and called horrible names to his understanding that his wife is giving birth to his child and that he is responsible for what she is experiencing. He can secretly thank God that he is a man and immune from this particular experience, but he should not gloat or show any signs that he lacks sympathy.

He should rather think about some of the sensual experiences he has shared with his wife and the promise that there will be more in the future. This is a crucial time. Although his wife might not consciously remember much, she will tuck it into her memory for future reference when the opportunity to rub it in his face presents itself. Second stage labor is not a very sensual time. But it is a good time to think loving thoughts.

The second stage of labor can last four to six hours. This is a long time for a husband to tolerate erratic slurs. This is what separates the good husbands from the mediocre. Be patient, be supportive, be loving, and when necessary, be scarce. If you have supportive nurses or a doula you really don't need to be in the delivery room the entire time your wife is in this transition labor. Make sure you have discussed this ahead of time. Explain that she might not want you there so she doesn't feel you have abandoned her.

Before you go any farther than the waiting room, make sure you have a sense of how far along the labor has progressed. If you are in the hospital cafeteria when your wife is ready to push, you may as well hail a cab and keep on going. Not a good thing to do. No matter what good you do in your life, no woman will forget if you miss the actual birth. Unless you are stuck overseas in an aircraft carrier or some other legitimate excuse, if you are not there for pushing and delivery, you may as well go into the witness protection program.

When your wife is fully dilated and effaced, which means that she is ready to give birth, she will be asked to push. This is an exciting time but can be very tiring for your wife. This is when you might want to take a strategic position out of direct sight. But be aware that this is what you have been waiting for. This is the reward. This is the moment.

After the baby is born and you return to your body, you need to be aware that your wife's job isn't quite done. She will need to deliver the placenta and she may need stitches. This is not a pretty sight either, so unless she asks for you (you can discuss this ahead of time), you might want to hang out with the nurses who are caring for the baby. If they have put the baby on your wife's chest, which is very common, find a good place to stand or take the opportunity to call your relatives. The birth experience can be joyous, sensual, and beautiful without your needing to gross yourself out.

After the baby is born, Mom and baby will likely spend a day or two in the hospital. This is a time for Mom to be treated as a goddess. It is important for Dad to bring a gift of some sort. Flowers are lovely. If you buy something for the baby like a stuffed animal, make sure you buy something equally cute for your wife. Don't forget that as much as you're anxious about her becoming a mother and paying all her attention to the baby, she is worried that you will no longer see her as your special one.

When a baby is born you want to make sure that neither of you are eclipsed by the birth. So pay extra attention to each other. It is a good idea for a husband to do something special and personal for his wife. Even a card with a special and romantic sentiment or a sexy sentiment will go a long way. As you transition into the realities of parenthood you want to savor these first few days and hours when you are in the afterglow. Soon enough the attention will be turned to other people and you will return to your life. Your routine will be new but you will have to face all the responsibilities and challenges you had before the birth.

When it is time to bring baby and Mom home from the hospital, make it sacred and special. Don't just let the occasion pass like any old day. You are bringing a baby home. Celebrate. Drink sparkling cider or a small amount of wine if the doctor says the nursing mom can have it. Have a special coming home meal.

Decorate the bedroom where Mom will continue to convalesce with a rocking chair and a special blanket. Treat everything as special and it will be. Take plenty of photographs. Talk baby talk to the baby and to each other.

Easing Back into Sex After Birth

Most likely, you won't be able to engage in sexual intercourse for at least six weeks after the baby is born. Your obstetrician will tell you when it is okay. But don't let this time mean that there is no sexual contact between you. Even though sex may be the last thing on the mom's mind, this is a very good time to connect in intimate ways that do not necessarily lead to sex.

The mom's breasts may be overly sensitive at this time so it may not be a good breast opportunity. When a mother is nursing she gets a feeling called a "letdown." It makes the breast fill with milk. If there is too much stimulation between feedings, especially as the milk and feeding schedule is regulating, the milk could let down and the breasts could become engorged.

Some women enjoy their breasts being fondled at this time. This is certainly a time when women are most feminine. Her breasts are full and are likely to be very sexy. You may just want to explore what feels good and what doesn't. Eventually everything will balance out and you will be able to play like you have been used to. Husbands should not get jealous of their babies. Nursing is the most natural and healthy way to feed an infant. The breasts will return to you in due time.

It is a good idea to stay connected even though you can't have sex. The longer you avoid it the more you will become nervous about it. When the mother has her six-week checkup and is given a green light to go ahead and resume normal sexual activity, her first reaction might be, "What, are you crazy?"

It is difficult for a woman to make the immediate transition to becoming sexual again when the memory of childbirth is still so fresh in her mind. She may also have memories of a sore rear end or any of the other lovely side effects of the process.

Even when the wife comes home and assures her husband that she is good to go, he might not be so anxious to give it a spin. He went through the process too. He may be afraid of hurting his wife. Or he might not have adjusted emotionally to the new circumstances.

Like anything else that has to do with sex, it is best to start out slowly. Caressing, touching, massaging, and gently exploring the genital area is the best way to get back on track. Be very aware, however, that even though the baby is a newborn, you can get pregnant again. When a woman nurses it may prevent pregnancy, but it is not a total guarantee. Ask your doctor and see what he or she recommends.

Be creative in getting back in touch with your sexuality. You no longer have the belly to contend with. But a woman's body changes after childbirth and she may take some time getting used to her new self. Men and women are often under the impression that everything will snap back into place immediately. It is important for women not to judge their changing shape as anything less than sexy. So much of sexiness is how you feel about yourself. If you are uncomfortable with how you look, you are not going to be able to let go and enjoy your loving.

Husbands should be just as reassuring now as they were when the belly was big. This is actually a time for *more* reassurance. The belly is gone but some of the weight will still be there. Some women lose it right away, some may take up to a year, and some women may find that their shapes remain altered. It will be to your vast advantage to tell your wife how sexy she is right now whether or not she ever changes a thing.

Sex and intimacy exist far beyond a physical connection. You are a couple and you are now a family. Your sexual relationship should be nurtured and loved as much as you nurture and love your new child. If you remember to be connected as lovers before, during, and after the birth of your baby, you will have experienced the process of sensual birth.

Chapter Nine shows you how to reclaim your passion now that you are parents and partners.

Chapter Nine

Reclaiming Passion: Parents and Partners

Your partner tenderly places your little bundle of joy into the infant car seat and secures all the straps and buckles. He gives the baby a kiss on the head, slides into the driver's seat, and gives you a big kiss on the lips for your first car ride as a family. As you drive through your neighborhood and pull up in front of your home, everything looks different. It's as if you are seeing your world for the first time. You're exhausted, but you're on cloud nine. You've never been happier or more in love.

Until, that is, your hormones bottom out and the reality of your situation hits you smack in the face like a wet towel. "Oh my God! What have we done?" is not an uncommon thought for the parents of newborns—especially if it's your first child. The last hurdle that couples must overcome in learning to stay lovers while being parents is the obvious one: the very presence of the baby.

While raising a child together can ultimately give a couple a deeper sense of "we," the initial birth of the baby tends to create more division in partnerships then it does unity. Rather than feeling "closer together than ever," couples often dwell on their differences. In the vast majority of relationships, these "differences" have existed all along, or for some time, but they don't become obvious until soon after the first child is born. If you approach your differences with an either/or attitude, someone wins and someone loses. It's smarter to work as a team. No matter what the obstacle is, find a way to solve it together. It's the *process of parenting* that creates a deeper connection between partners, not the acts of conception or giving birth. Learning to improve your communications skills— speaking *and* listening, solving problems, compromising—are critical to your success. Facing the obstacles head-on can be overwhelming, but ignoring a problem will almost always make it worse. Each hurdle you clear as a couple gives you more faith in yourselves, each other, and your relationship.

The juggling act that many parents perform in order to fit everything in, and get everything done, is quite impressive—but it's all for nought, unless giving time and energy to each other as mates is part of this daily picture. Some parents mistakenly believe that it is their responsibility always to put the baby first—no matter what. If you want your relationship to be going strong when Junior goes off to college, I suggest that you rethink this idea. Of course, you must take care of your baby's needs, and most of the time you'll want to put him or her first. However, if you do not give equal time and energy to nourishing your partnership, everyone will suffer and the child you are sacrificing your relationship for will often be affected more negatively than everyone else involved.

According to a study conducted by Jay Belsky, author of *The Transition to Parenthood: How a First Child Changes a Marriage,* the more satisfied parents are with their relationship, the better off their child or children tend to be. Belsky says, "Marital satisfaction does influence parental competence . . . broadly speaking, we found that the more a marriage satisfies an individual's needs and desires, the less likely the individual is to insert those needs and desires in appropriately into the parent-child relationship."

Once the first or second child is born, many relationships appear to simply fall apart. This tends to happen predominantly with couples who say they have "lost their connection" or "fallen out of love." When you look closely at these couples, what you often discover is that during the pregnancy or after the birth of the child, one or both of them stopped making sexual activity a priority. In fact, according to a survey conducted by *L.A. Parent* magazine, a couple's frequency of sexual activity plummets after the birth of their first baby. The survey results showed that the percentage of couples who made love three or more times a week fell from 54 percent before having children to only 5 percent afterward. Well, no wonder marital satisfaction often drops after having children!

Ironically, rarely does a medical or physical reason prevent a couple from resuming their sex life once the woman has completely recovered from giving birth. There *are* hormones that depress a woman's libido, but these stabilize again shortly after birth, or for breast-feeding women, whenever they stop nursing. Of course, fatigue can stop the most willing woman in her tracks, but if you care about maintaining a healthy relationship, you have to learn how to manage your time, get your rest, and delegate as much as you possibly can. No one is going to make time for you to have sex. And if you don't have sex, sooner or later, you will wake up and find out that you're no longer lovers.

So, how do you join the "Parents Club" without turning in your membership card to "Lovers for Life"?

First, let's hope you've been following my guidance and have continued to have an active sex life throughout the pregnancy, because this really helps couples to make the transition more smoothly.

Second, you make the heartfelt commitment to yourselves, and to each other, that you will remain lovers and continue to enjoy the passion and intimacy that only making love can create and maintain.

Third, you question the mind-set of the majority of couples who stop making sex a priority. When there are no physical barriers, the roadblocks are generally mental or emotional. That means that something you have learned or experienced in your life is creating a belief that you can't or shouldn't continue being lovers once you're parents. I challenge you to find any good reason why this myth should rule your future together!

And fourth, by becoming aware of the changes and challenges that are on the way and learning how to deal with them now, you will be able to navigate the twists and turns of parenthood and become even closer as a couple.

Once you've taken the first three steps, you're ready to learn about the challenges that come part and parcel with parenthood. First of all, it's important to know that aside from societal stereotypes that may be influencing you, the act of becoming parents is one of the most life-altering experiences that you can have. Parenthood turns you into different people, both mentally and emotionally. For a woman, the differences are physical, too. So, in essence, having a child does transform who you both are as individuals. The good news is that your love life can not only survive this transition, it can flourish.

When Can We Start Having Sex Again?

Every woman is different, but many obstetricians suggest waiting at least six weeks after the child is born before you resume sexual intercourse. This advice is given in order to prevent an infection, but some doctors say that it's simply a remnant of earlier days when infections were life threatening because effective antibiotics were not readily available. However, many doctors still automatically schedule a woman's postpartum checkup for six weeks after the baby is born and generally tell her to refrain from intercourse until he or she gives the "all clear."

I suggest you schedule your appointment for one month after you deliver. It's likely that if you had a healthy pregnancy, and if you didn't need an episiotomy, your body will be physically healed enough to resume sex within four weeks. Of course, even if you get the green light at four weeks, it doesn't mean you have to resume intercourse right away. The nice thing is that you'll know it's safe if you choose to do it. If your doctor tells you to hold off for another week or so, and you were hoping to get the go-ahead, you can use this time period to fantasize and build up your desire, so that when *can* do it, you'll be ready, willing, and able!

Those of you who have had an episiotomy may also be healed at the four-week point, but don't push the envelope here. Make sure you really are completely healed and that all tenderness has subsided before you have sex with penetration. One way to get an indication as to whether or not you're ready is to press on the opening of your vagina. (Obviously, you don't even want to try this "test" until you no longer feel pain or discomfort in your everyday movements.) If pressing on the opening of your vagina feels uncomfortable, you're not ready.

If you are one of many women who choose to wait six weeks or more after giving birth to have intercourse again, that's perfectly understandable. You are the only one who knows how your body is feeling. However, the longer you put off intercourse, the more important it will be to connect intimately through other forms of sex, or by using some of the intimacy alternatives offered in Chapter Seven.

Navigating Through the Top Ten Roadblocks to Postpartum Passion

1.   Postpartum Blues

By about four days after you give birth, your "pregnancy hormones" will have dropped tenfold. The fact that your body is doing exactly what it's supposed to do is very little consolation when you can't stop crying, feeling anxious, or being cranky. These mood swings, or emotional lows, are called the baby blues, because so many women feel sad and weepy when the hormones nose-dive. These feelings should decrease as your hormone levels return to normal. However, it can take anywhere from several days to several weeks for your hormones to level out, so hang in there! Meanwhile, don't assume that you're "the only one going through this." More than 50 percent of new fathers experience their own version of the baby blues, so your mate might be struggling with his own feelings as well.

Obviously, the more you can rest during this time, the better, but make sure you're getting up and moving around a little, just to keep the blood circulating. Some of the depressed feelings are exaggerated because your body is so depleted. Make it a point to ask your doctor to recommend a multivitamin and take it as faithfully as you took your pregnancy vitamins.

If you feel like crying, cry. Don't try to suppress your emotions or convince yourself that you're okay when you are not. Crying is a wonderful way to release stress, increase your oxygen intake, and relax your muscles. If you can take a nap or go to bed for the night after a "good cry," that's even better. You'll sleep very soundly, and this is the perfect time for your mate to get up and tend to the baby's needs while you get some much-deserved dreamtime.

If the baby blues last longer than a few weeks, talk with a professional. If you're one of the 10 percent of women who suffer from an actual postpartum depression, the sooner it's diagnosed, the better off you, your partner, and your baby will be. There are many effective ways to treat this condition, but getting help is essential. Do not wait for things to magically turn around by themselves.

2. Fatigue

The number one reason that couples give for having little or no sex after they have their first baby is fatigue—often bordering on exhaustion. Sheldon H. Cherry, obstetrician/gynecologist, estimated that a woman uses as much energy giving birth as she would if she hiked a twelve-mile trail. That's a lot of energy! In addition, if this is your first baby, or if this birth had complications, you are probably feeling some anxiety about your ability to meet all of the new demands. Add to this the general sleep deprivations that most parents face with newborns, and it's no wonder you feel like you can never get enough rest.

Unlike physical activities such as washing dishes, making beds, or running the vacuum cleaner, which burn up energy, satisfying sex can actually replenish your energy reserves. Having good sex on a regular basis also strengthens your immune system and helps you to sleep more soundly. Orgasms have been proven to relieve aches and pains, including headaches. So the next time you feel a headache coming on, instead of saying "no" to sex, initiate it. The same goes for stress. If you feel too stressed out to have sex, having sex is one of the best things you can do! I realize that this may go against logic, but very often in life the things that we're avoiding are the things that are actually good for us in some way.

If friends and relatives ask you for gift suggestions, I highly recommend asking for gift certificates for meals and services. Especially when you're exhausted, having dinner delivered and having someone come in to clean the house, do the laundry, and run errands can be a godsend! Massage gift certificates are wonderful too.

As far as combating the fatigue goes, make sure you're getting the proper nutrition, and in particular enough iron. There's nothing like pregnancy and childbirth to deplete your body's reserves of iron, so continue taking your vitamins and also eat more foods that are rich in iron. A few of the foods highest in iron are broccoli, chicken, spinach, and other leafy greens such as kale and collard greens.

3. Physical Body Changes

Your body and mind will experience more upheaval in the six weeks after your baby is born than at any other time in your life. This happens because all of the changes that your body made over the nine months to prepare for the birth of a healthy baby are suddenly reversed. Whereas it took three-quarters of a year to get to this point, returning to a state where pregnancy is physically possible again can happen within months.

An example of one of the many changes your body is making is the amount of weight that you lose in the month after you give birth. According to medical research and studies, if a woman were to lose this much weight at any other time of her life, her body would go into a state of physical shock.

The first six weeks after birth are frequently referred to as the "post-partum recovery period," and it is during this time frame that a new mother's reproductive organs resume their nonpregnant state. But that doesn't mean that within two months everything will be back to normal.

First of all, some of the changes, such as stretch marks, are here to stay. They'll eventually fade to your natural skin color, but the indentations are permanent. No amount of creams or magic potions can reduce stretch marks. These products are great when it comes to making your skin feel more comfortable, but stretch marks are the result of ligaments that are in the deep layers of the skin, so there's really not much you can do about them.

Another permanent change is that your uterus is sitting lower in the pelvic girdle than it did prior to pregnancy. The degree to which it "sinks" depends on how much the ligaments stretched and how well they are able to "shrink back." In rare cases, the uterus drops so low into the pelvis that it actually sinks into the vagina. This is called a "prolapsed uterus" and happens most often with women who have had three or more vaginal deliveries.

One of the most surprising physical factors for new parents is that the baby's mother will still look pregnant for a couple of weeks (or more) after giving birth, but this will soon pass! The other temporary conditions of pregnancy and childbirth, such as hemorrhoids and vaginal discomfort, generally start to subside within a month or so, but they can linger for several months up to a year for some women.

Your Changing Breasts

"You see, I have run, stepped, lifted weights, and stretched in gyms all over town, but the inches that were once part of my breasts are now firmly attached to my waist."

Neysa Whiteman, M.D.
The New Mother's Body Book

During the first few days after your baby is born, the "milk" that comes out of your breasts is actually a substance called "colostrum." This nutritional substance is one of the best gifts a mother can give to a newborn, because it is not only full of vitamins and minerals, it also contains important antibodies, and some research suggests that it can help to prevent many types of allergies.

After about four days, the real milk will begin to flow into your breasts, and the most dramatic increase in breast size happens at this time. The milk-producing hormones and swelling in your breast tissue will make your breasts feel almost pendulous, and for many women, painful. Take heart. The initial discomfort or pain is the worst part of it and that's usually over within twenty-four hours.

In the meantime, if you plan to breast-feed, you can use warm compresses to ease the pain and encourage the milk to flow out of your breasts. The soft rubber form of hot water bottles work well, too, and so does standing in a hot shower and letting the water cascade down over your breasts. It's a good idea to invest in a manual breast pump before you have your baby, so you're prepared to relieve the engorgement by hand-expressing some of your milk. Gently, but firmly massaging your breasts from the top, down toward the nipples can also stimulate the "letdown" effect and cause the milk to start flowing.

If you're not planning to breast-feed, use ice packs or bags of frozen peas to ease the discomfort instead of heat. Tempted as you might be, resist the urge to squeeze milk out of your breasts, because this will stimulate more milk production. Your doctor may prescribe a drug to help dry up the milk. Be sure to ask about possible side effects if you choose this alternative.

Whether you breast-feed or not, many women complain of sore nipples during pregnancy and after giving birth. One of the best remedies

I've come across is pure vitamin E oil. Just a drop on each nipple will soothe and help your tender skin to heal.

One of the perks of breast-feeding is that the likelihood of ovulating is usually suppressed for as long as you continue. This is part of your body's way of ensuring that you don't conceive again too soon. Meanwhile, if you don't breast-feed, you will probably start menstruating again in a few months. Unless you want to get pregnant again right away, be sure to get back into your birth control practices.

After-Pains and Lingering Discomforts

Most women experience what are called "after-pains" for a few days to a week after the baby is born. These are caused by your uterus contracting in order to expel any remaining blood or fragments of placenta. The contractions generally only last a minute or less, but they can be fairly uncomfortable or surprisingly powerful for some women.

Meanwhile, your bulging uterus that was recently so apparent will, within two weeks, be difficult to locate. During the first six weeks after you give birth, your uterus shrinks from about 2 pounds to about 2 ounces. It actually gets about 20 times smaller than it was at the end of your term.

If you have managed to escape hemorrhoids throughout your pregnancy, it's likely that the act of giving birth has caused you to join the ranks of those who have already been intimately introduced to these small, yet powerful pains in the butt. According to a study conducted by the makers of Preparation H, 70 percent of women have hemorrhoids some time during their pregnancy or as a result of their delivery. I suggest a hemorrhoid ointment that has cortisone in it and these are available without a prescription. A home remedy for hemorrhoids is the fresh gel from an Aloe Vera plant. (See Chapter Five for more information on how to use Aloe Vera.)

Remember a few weeks ago when you wished you didn't have to run to the bathroom so frequently to urinate? Well, that wish is probably coming true now, and if you're like most women, you're not enjoying it. It takes several weeks for your bladder and urethra to resume their "prepregnant" position and state of operations. Just keep drinking plenty of pure, fresh water and nature will take care of the rest.

Unfortunately, those of you who have had an episiotomy will suffer a few additional complaints when it comes to urinating. Common complaints from women who have had this procedure include pain, swelling, and itching.

In addition, women who undergo episiotomies often say that intercourse is uncomfortable, painful, or entirely out of the question for at least three or four months.

Most doctors recommend that women who have had episiotomies wear an ice pack for at least the first day. This will help reduce the swelling and ease some of the discomfort. One of the best makeshift ice packs are small bags of frozen peas. Buy a few bags so you can always have a bag in the freezer and ready to go. I learned this trick from an athlete who uses the large bags of peas to ice his legs after running. The peas allow the "ice pack" to conform to your body and when they start to defrost, they don't actually melt like ice, so there's no concern about water leakage. When the bag stops feeling cold, pop it back in the freezer and pull out one of your reserves.

It is also a good idea to use an anesthetic cream or spray. If your doctor doesn't suggest one, ask for some recommendations. The home remedy, which still works well, is gauze pads soaked in witch hazel. A friend's grandmother said she used to fill a canning jar with square pieces of gauze, pour in witch hazel, and put the jar in the icebox to guarantee an extra cool sensation each time she reapplied the remedy. Witch hazel is good for itching and soreness too.

Your Vagina

If you deliver vaginally, there *do* tend to be some permanent changes in size and shape, but most couples agree that the differences are not that obvious until the woman has had two or more children. Another difference that you will notice is a decrease in the amount of moisture. This happens because estrogen levels, which help your vaginal walls create lubrication, drop dramatically after childbirth. The lower levels of estrogen can also result in thinning of the vaginal walls. These changes generally last for several weeks to a month for women who are not breast-feeding, and for those who *do* breast-feed, estrogen levels will stay low for as long as you nurse your baby. These changes do not have to have a negative impact on your lovemaking, so long as you are both aware of what's going on and make allowances. For example, get used to keeping a tube of K-Y jelly or Astroglide next to the bed, or better yet, a small jar of pure olive or almond oil.

If you and your partner have previously enjoyed the feel of deep thrusting during intercourse, you might want to ease off on the amount of pressure you are using. This really has to be the woman's call. If you say it hurts or it feels uncomfortable, then your partner has to stop and let you redirect him. Sometimes simply shifting to a different position can turn pain into delightful pleasure, so experiment and see what works for you. If penetration doesn't feel good in any position at the moment, use a lubricant and give him a firm "hand job."

4. The Parent Trap

Both the man and the woman can potentially suffer from this roadblock: giving priority to being parents rather than lovers. This often occurs in the shift that people go through when they have children, thinking that since they are now adults, they must act like "parents," which equates to being sexless, homogenized, and stiff—which I call the "Ward and June Cleaver" syndrome. Meanwhile, the very presence of the baby nearby serves to reinforce the loss of spontaneity and freedom the couple once had. It is imperative for couples to avoid this powerful deterrent to maintaining intimacy after pregnancy.

Just being aware of this potential problem tips the scales in your favor. For many couples, the parent trap kind of creeps up on them without them realizing it and subpsychologically they start to view each other as parents instead of lovers. There's nothing really sexy about stereotypical parents. Think about the images that are portrayed on television. For the most part, parents are depicted as anything but sexy and often come off as asexual. The "mother" wears a nice sweater with a shirt tucked under it and has a bobbed hairdo. The "father" is kind of dumpy with his baggy pants and clean-cut look. They're never shown as sexual creatures. And so the message that we get, not only from the way that we're feeling, but reinforced by the media, is that parents aren't sexy.

If you don't maintain your roles as lovers throughout the pregnancy, it's highly likely that there's going to suddenly be this feeling of, "What happened to us?" "We're not attracted to each other." "We're not having sex anymore." These feelings, especially in light of the fact that you now have a new life to care for, can create a real sense of panic. The fears and anxieties trigger arguments and polarization, wherein each person is blaming the other. "He doesn't understand that I'm tired." "She doesn't understand that I have needs." By knowing that these thoughts and feelings are natural, and that they are not personal, we can respond much more rationally and effectively. Even when you don't understand each other, you have to be willing to express your love and desire for each other. By doing this, you maintain your link as lovers, and the strength of your teamwork improves.

5.   A Woman's Lack of Desire

Evidence suggests that a woman's diminished desire for sex after giving birth is directly linked to—you guessed it—hormones! This seems to be particularly true for women who are nursing. When you're breast-feeding, your body is in a semimenopausal state. The hormone, prolactin, which is needed to produce breast milk, suppresses some of the hormones that normally would be triggering sexual desire. Some experts go so far as to say that a woman who is nursing is in a state of "asexuality" and simply doesn't possess the urge to have sex. Other authorities, such as Tracy Hotchner, author of *Pregnancy and Childbirth,* reported that women who breast-feed have more frequent orgasms that are often more powerful and satisfying. According to Hotchner, "The [breast-feeding] hormones enlarge your veins and promote growth of new blood vessels in your pelvis. This raises the response potential of your vagina and clitoris."

So, the down side is that you may not want to have sex, and the up side is that if you do, it can be incredible!

It's very important to understand, however, that there are very good reasons for a woman's hormones to suppress her sexual desire for a time period of months to a year after she gives birth. It is actually nature's way of making sure that she doesn't get pregnant again too soon.

History shows us that these "safeguards" date back to prehistoric times, when humans lived nomadic lives. In the days of big game hunting, a tribe had to follow the herds of animals that provided their main food and fuel sources. They didn't have horses, so they had to walk and carry all of their possessions. Children, younger than two or three years old, who could not keep up with the herd, had to be carried. This is one of the reasons why a woman's body discourages her desire for sex for as long as she is nursing a baby. A woman could only carry one child at a time, and typically only produced enough milk to adequately feed one at a time.

Knowing the causes of a decreased libido helps couples to understand that it's not personal, it's actually Mother Nature's way of increasing the baby's chances for survival! Even if your partner knows this, he will need to be reassured that you are not rejecting him and that you still find him attractive and sexy.

Physical Deterrents

Even if a woman *does* have a desire for sex in the weeks after she delivers, the state of her body may discourage her from taking action. For example, it's normal to have a bloody discharge for between three and six weeks after the baby is born. This is called "lochia" and is the blood from the point where the placenta detached from the uterus, the lining of the uterus, and small pieces of the placenta that were not expelled during the after-birth. The average amount of lochia is only about a pint and most of that is expelled within four days after birth, but you may find this hard to believe as you open yet another box of sanitary pads. (**Note:** Most doctors agree that nothing should be inserted into the vagina while the cervix is still so open, and that includes tampons. This precaution should be heeded to avoid a nasty uterine infection and plenty of discomfort. It takes about ten days for your cervix to return to its normal size.)

You should also take it really slow for at least an entire week after you give birth. Too much activity can cause excess bleeding because your uterus hasn't had time to recover yet.

If you're not accustomed to using pads, especially the supersized ones that you'll need for a few days, you may feel like you're walking around with a mattress between your legs. Just hang in there for a few days, and you'll be able to switch to a pad that's a little less bulky. Changing pads frequently will help you to feel fresher and increase your comfort level. Meanwhile, if the flow is so heavy that you have to change pads two or more times in an hour, you need to slow way down and call your doctor for further instructions. Other reasons to call your physician include itching, or a foul odor, puss, and large clots of blood. Generally speaking lochia will be bright red after birth, turn to a rust color after a week or two, and then fade to a yellow or nearly clear color. If however, you see bright red blood again—after it has already changed to a brownish color, that's an indication that should be reported to your doctor.

Self-Image Issues

Many women, who used to love the way their bodies looked, are now confronted with the reality that some things are not going to return to their "pre-pregnant" state. Unfortunately, this reality seems bleak to multitudes of women because they have been sold on the idea that a young-looking, thin body is the epitome of sexiness. What I hear from women is that the permanent effects on their bodies, such as stretch marks on the breasts, wider hips, or more cellulite, make them feel less appealing.

I suggest working together as a team to jump this hurdle. First of all, it's very valuable for a woman to see images of pregnant women and mothers who are depicted as powerful, rather than "out of shape." Many ancient cultures revered motherhood and depicted mothers as women with grace, power, and wisdom. By expanding your idea of what's sexy and what's not, it will be easier for you to believe that these changes do not have to take away from your desirability or sex appeal.

Second, it's vital that your mate help you to get over this hump by appreciating and acknowledging your body exactly as it is right now. If a woman has a partner who's saying, "Well, it's okay, honey. You'll get back in shape. You'll look as good as you did before," he's essentially sending the message that this new form is not acceptable. It doesn't take a brain surgeon to figure out that these kinds of comments just make a woman feel worse, and potentially resentful to boot!

And speaking of resentment . . . that's a big intimacy killer in itself! Some women aren't interested in having sex because they're harboring resentment for their mates. These women say that their partners are not giving them enough help or are acting like having a baby is no big deal. One woman's husband actually said, "It's been two months. Shouldn't you be over it by now?" Fortunately, comments like these are usually made out of ignorance rather than malice. Instead of hitting him over the head with a brick, educate him. When he really understands what your body has gone through, he will most likely be amazed. It's best if this education begins early in your pregnancy, but if it hasn't been happening all along, don't waste any time now. Assuming that the two of you are having a loving relationship, the more he understands what you're going through, the more he'll want to give you the help and support that you need.

6.   A Man's Lack of Desire

In most cases, thanks to hormones and Mother Nature, it's more common for a woman to experience a drop in libido after having a child than it is for her partner's desire to wane. However, a lot of men do experience a dip in their desires, and this can be attributed to a number of different factors.

For some men, the stress and responsibility of becoming a father can be enough to nip their arousal in the bud. For men who are actively involved in taking care of the baby and doing household chores, exhaustion and fatigue will be in constant competition with their sexual desires. Other men are affected by their idea of what "daddy" means and may suddenly think that being sexy and flirtatious is not appropriate. All of these issues can be worked through and resolved, though it will probably take some time.

Meanwhile, many women don't want to hear this, but the men who often have the most difficulty awakening their desire for sexual intercourse are the ones who watched their babies being born. In one study, 30 percent of men who witnessed the birth of their baby later experienced some degree of impotence. This study, conducted by Sam Janus of New York Medical College, Valhalla, New York, supports the feedback that I have heard from numerous men who witnessed the birth of their babies. This statistic is based on the number of men who were positioned down by the vagina, not those who stayed by their mate's side during delivery.

In addition, most of the women I've talked to say their partner is much more helpful if he stays up by her side. One woman told me, "I was exhausted and it took everything to push. I wanted my husband right next to me. He was behind the doctor and when I called him, he actually said, 'Wait, I don't want to miss this part.' I wanted to kill him."

Some men also experience a loss of libido because they feel responsible for putting their mates through the pains of pregnancy and childbirth, or they are afraid that their partners are not healed enough yet to make it okay. These are obstacles that can almost always be talked through—either privately or with a professional.

7.   Breastfeeding Jealousy or Awkwardness

Many men admit that they feel threatened or left out when their mate nurses the baby. For some men, breast-feeding may be a constant reminder that their partners' breasts are no longer reserved just for them, and that these "sex toys" have a biological function. Other men report feeling threatened or left out when their partners nurse the baby. These feelings tend to be confirmed when a man's mate suddenly no longer wants him to touch or fondle her breasts.

This is a case for education and clear communication. First of all, if you are going through this, or suspect that you might be, make sure your partner knows what's biologically and physically happening with your breasts. This will help him to understand that you're not rejecting him and that this is a temporary situation.

If you are one of the many breast-feeding women who feel overtouched, and thus are disinterested in having your breasts fondled, explain this to your mate. Also tell him that having your breasts stimulated can cause them to become engorged and uncomfortable.

Meanwhile, since arousing the breast is one of the things that makes the milk flow out, it's not unusual for a woman's breasts to start releasing milk when her partner kisses or fondles them. Even if your mate is comfortable with your choice to nurse your baby, and has watched and helped you to do it, there's a good chance he'll be set back a few paces by a milk-squirting breast. Try to keep a sense of humor about this. A lot of couples just work around the breasts until the breast-feeding stage is over. I suggest to men that they gently kiss their partner's breasts, just to stay connected with them and to show they still find them sexy, but not in an attempt to stimulate them, unless their partner wants them to be stimulated.

Allowing—and playfully encouraging—your partner to gently cup your breasts in his hands and give them an occasional kiss lets him know that you are still his. Many men feel like their nursing partners' breasts are suddenly "off limits" to them and that their position as "one and only," has been overtaken. Even the most rational man can experience a bout of breast-feeding jealousy and it is actually far more common than you may think.

8. Living on Autopilot

Once the baby is born, many couples find themselves living a monotonous life on automatic pilot, as they go from a full day of work, then home to take care of the baby, and back to work the next morning. With this routine, the couple never manages to devote time to themselves, each other, or keeping their romance alive.

If this scenario sounds all too familiar to you, I suggest that within one week you begin developing the following habits.

Me Time

Every day, you and your mate give each other thirty minutes of "responsibility-free" time to use however you please. That means that he takes care of the baby while you rest, nap, read, talk on the phone, or whatever you feel like doing, and vice versa. Most couples find it helpful to pick the same time to do this each day, if only to avoid having one more thing to schedule! The important point here is that each of you gets to pick the thirty minutes that you would most like to have—which may not be the half-hour your mate is hoping you choose, or vice versa.

The reason that "Me Time" is so important is that unless both you and your mate have some time to yourself every day, you're not going to have quality time with each other. Practicing Me Time is also a great way for couples to show each other that they care about each other.

In addition to the thirty minutes each day, I highly recommend that you give each other at least a half day of Me Time once a month.

We Time

Every day, in addition to sharing two thirty-second "love connections," I suggest that you devote thirty minutes to nurturing your relationship. Just like Me Time, the thirty minutes you choose for "We Time" should be scheduled in advance, and you're more likely to honor this commitment if it happens at about the same time every day.

Some couples love connecting over coffee and breakfast, while others reserve thirty minutes in bed each night to snuggle, talk, and just be completely present with each other. Obviously this works the best if the baby doesn't interrupt with his or her own needs. However, if your baby cries, or needs something, tend to its needs, and then move your focus back to the "we" of your partnership as quickly as possible.

At least once a month, hire a baby-sitter so that you and your mate can share at least five hours of uninterrupted We Time.

I don't recommend that We Time automatically include sex, but I do suggest that you are open to the possibility each time. Some couples report that their daily We Time is an opportunity to build up sexual urgency and tension with small doses of fondling and foreplay. After the urge builds for a few days, they both have an increased desire to satisfy their desire. Whereas foreplay used to be a twenty- to thirty-minute time block, followed by lovemaking, now it might be one or two minutes at a time over the course of several days—finally followed—thank goodness—by satisfying sex!

9.   Burning the Midnight Oil

This roadblock reflects the fact that many couples work more than one job while raising a family. Whether it's the woman or the man—or both—who work nonstop, many couples are simply too exhausted after a long day at work, followed by even more hours at home doing errands and chores just to keep the homestead running. Some couples might even have opposing schedules, with one partner working days, the other nights. When burning the midnight oil becomes their way of life, it is likely that the couple will find it nearly impossible to make time for each other, and so they must learn how to break this cycle.

Breaking this cycle generally means making numerous small changes or one or two whoppers. You may need to consider changing jobs or transferring into a department that offers more flexible hours. Some couples decide to move closer to family members who are willing and able to help out with child care and household responsibilities. Many couples discover that they can stop moonlighting if they simplify their lives or consolidate their debts.

The bottom line is that you have to get creative and come up with a way to honor your highest priorities, such as keeping your partnership strong and raising your child together.

10.   Emotional Challenges

I doubt if there's a single couple who has had a baby without going through some sort of emotional stress or turmoil. With so many changes happening all at once, people are bound to experience a wide range of emotions. Once again, the key is to work through these emotional challenges as a team, rather than pitting yourself against each other or playing tit for tat. It's not about "being right." It's about taking care of each other and your relationship so you can remain lovers and raise an emotionally secure child.

For women, one of the biggest emotional challenges is a sense of feeling overwhelmed and "underhelped." Not only can this lead to resentment and a lack of sexual desire, as I explained earlier, but it can also fester into long-standing grudges. If you feel like you're marching uphill alone, chances are that you need to be heard and understood, just as much as you need to be helped. Explain to your partner that you don't expect him to solve every problem or pick up all the slack. You just want him to show his support by listening and then teaming up with you to come up with options and solutions. Also, let him know that you want to play this same role for him and the challenges that he's facing.

For men, the biggest emotional hurdles have to do with feeling left out, or less important. According to a variety of studies, this is the number one reason why men stray into affairs shortly after their mates give birth. What's ironic is that many times a woman who has just borne a man a child, loves him, and needs him more than ever—and just isn't focused on showing it. I encourage women to make it a point to show their husbands how much they need and love them by putting a little note in his briefcase or lunchbox or picking up his favorite dessert when you drive by the bakery.

Men also complain that instead of getting to help care for the baby, or for their partner, they end up with all the drudgery jobs such as cleaning, dishes, grocery shopping, and errands. Some men take this as a personal insult, and they feel as if their partners don't trust them with the baby.

Obviously, since everyone is different, we all face different emotional challenges and obstacles as we go through the transition to parenting. Don't assume that you know what your partner is feeling; ask him. Don't expect your mate to know what you're feeling; tell him. You don't have to agree with each other, but you do have to respect each other's thoughts and opinions. Frequently remind yourself that you are both on the same team!

Tips for Reclaiming Your Passion

You deserve to enjoy all of the intimacy, passion, and heart-pounding pleasure that you've ever had, and you *can!* The key is to approach your sexual reunion as a fresh start, rather than a reenactment of what used to be. This mind-set will help smooth the way for more spontaneity, and it will also help you to avoid making comparisons. One of the mistakes that couples commonly make is to use their "pre-pregnancy sex" as a yardstick for measuring what happens after the baby is born. I suggest that you throw away the old yardstick, and start fresh. Undress each other slowly and appreciate each other. Proceed slowly and gently and stay alert for new sensations and responses.

It's also helpful to be more candid about planning time to have sex. If you set a "date" for 3:00 P.M. on Sunday afternoon, you both have something to look forward to throughout the week and you can reserve energy for the occasion. While spontaneity during sex is a wonderful thing, without making an appointment with your lover to have sex, the opportunity to be spontaneous may not occur.

As for the sex itself, you've already read about some of the bigger changes, but there are some subtle differences as well. For example, after a woman gives birth, her labia are "softer and fleshier" than they were before pregnancy. Many women say their labia remain more sensitive after giving birth and their pleasure, especially from oral sex, is increased.

Meanwhile, your vagina will gradually regain a good bit of your pre-pregnant feel and tone within a couple of months of giving birth, but it generally remains slightly larger that it was nine months ago. Some women say they enjoy intercourse more now, because of a more "relaxed" fit, and because the intensity of their sensitivity is up a few notches.

Although some men initially miss the old degree of "snugness," others say they prefer the new, fuller, more flexible feel of their mate's vagina. Most women can regain a great deal of their original shape and elasticity, and one of the best ways to do this is to continue doing your Kegel exercises. (If you don't know how to do the Kegel, refer to Chapter Five.) Doing Kegels can tone and tighten a loose vagina, help protect against a prolapsed uterus, help prevent urinary incontinence, and speed the recover from an episiotomy. I agree with the doctors who suggest doing 300 to 400 Kegels a day for the first several months after you deliver. After that, I recommend that you keep doing at least 10 a day for the rest of your life.

Some women have trouble isolating the pelvic floor muscles in order to contract and release them properly and get the full benefit of the Kegel exercise. Well, guess what? You can now buy "vaginal weights," for this inner workout. You simply insert the cone-shaped weight into your vagina the same way you insert a tampon. The weight feels like it's going to fall out, which automatically triggers the pelvic floor muscles to contract. These weights work so well that many women who use them while waiting to have surgery to correct urinary incontinence end up canceling the surgery because they no longer need it! Another great reason to add vaginal weights to your daily workout routine is that when your pelvic floor muscles are in tip-top shape, the intensity of your orgasms is significantly increased. (Don't start your "weight workouts" until after your doctor says it's safe to have intercourse again.)

Pump Up Your Passion Potential

The more proactive you both are about keeping your passion alive, the more connected you're going to feel, and the more you will continue to experience each other as lovers—even when the baby's in the next room. The following are a list of ideas to get you going. But don't stop there. Make your own list of "passion pumpers" and be the hottest parents on the block!

Get Out

Hire someone to care for your baby and get out of the house together for a few hours. Enjoy a meal together, see a steamy movie, sit in the park, or go for a drive. What you do doesn't matter as much as simply getting out of the atmosphere of your home, where at the moment you are predominantly Mommy and Daddy, and getting to be carefree lovers for an evening or an afternoon.

Sleep In

Every now and again, hire an "overnight sitter" or nanny and go spend the evening in a nearby hotel. Unless you're feeling particularly energetic, I suggest spending the evening relaxing, reading, or watching a movie in bed, followed by a great night of uninterrupted sleep. Then, take full advantage of the hotel's late checkout policy and spend a leisurely morning lounging, eating breakfast in bed, and having great sex!

Me Time and We Time

Continue making time for each other and your relationship. This often becomes even more important as your child grows up and begins to have an active life.

Afternoon Delight

If you're exhausted by the time you go to bed each night, give it a try in the afternoon. Some couples really enjoy cuddling up with each other on weekend afternoons as the baby naps. This can often lead to lovemaking, and it will certainly lead to a better bond and deeper intimacy within the couple.

Expand Your Repertoire

Make it a point to add something fresh to your sex life every few months. Try a new position, or add a toy to your adult playpen! I suggest you visit an adult sex store, or check out what's available online. If you've never shared or acted out your fantasies, there's no time like the present. I also recommend using quality erotica to heat up your engines. Men tend to prefer movies and women often enjoy reading passages from sexy romance novels. Variety adds spice, so mix it up.

If you and your partner are not enjoying sex within three months after the baby is born, seek professional help. Sometimes it turns out to be something relatively simple that can be resolved in a few visits. If it turns out to be something bigger, it's even more important to work it out now, before it snowballs.

Chapter Ten

Lovers for Life

It's a warm summer Sunday. You and your partner are relaxing on the front porch swing, reading the paper and sipping your coffee. Your twelve-year-old daughter, with baseball glove and ball in hand, announces that she's on her way to the park to play ball with the neighbors and promises to be back in time for dinner.

You and your mate share a knowing look and a smile. You both hop off the swing, letting the sections of newspaper drift to the floor and land where they may, and you head inside. You usually like to slowly undress each other, savoring every moment, but it's been more than a week since you've made love, so you unbutton your blouse and your mate wriggles out of his jeans while you make your way to the bedroom. You fall onto the bed, out of breath with desire, and spend the next hour in sex heaven!

If you're thinking, "Yeah, right!" or "That'll be the day" you're not the only one! In fact, most couples with a twelve-year-old child would probably continue reading the paper without the idea of having sex even crossing their minds. And that's one of the reasons why so many couples stop being lovers, even though they may still love each other. I wish I could give you a magic potion or formula that would quickly and easily keep this from happening, but the truth is that you have to put some energy into a relationship if you want to keep the love affair alive.

In my experience, the three most valuable forms of energy to invest in your relationship are time, thought, and talent.

Time

Spend quality couple's time together every day—even if it's only thirty minutes. Make arrangements for child care so you can share at least one uninterrupted three-hour time block of "We Time" each week.

Thought

Think about what you can do to please your mate and express the love and gratitude that you have for him or her. Put some thought into planning fun and intimate outings and minivacations ahead of time. (The list of Fifty Ways to Please Your Lover at the end of this chapter will be a big help with this one!)

Talent

Many people seem satisfied to be a sufficient or relatively skilled lover, but if you're partners for life, I suggest that you both commit to being the best, most talented lovers you can be. Technique isn't everything, but knowing about each other's bodies and how to elicit the most pleasurable responses will keep you both coming back for more!

Honing Your Talents

Creating the recommended amount of We Time and putting thought into your relationship on a regular basis are both new habits that, with practice and repetition, will eventually become a natural way of life. Not so with talent! I have yet to encounter someone with innate sexual talents, although we might all have a predisposition for being good at one thing or another. The key is to realize that no matter how good you are, as long as you're living and breathing, there's always more to learn and plenty of room for improvement. Make becoming a better lover a priority and I guarantee you that your efforts will pay off tenfold!

In order to improve a skill or polish a talent, you need a place to practice. I suggest that you take the necessary steps to turn your bedroom (or a guest room) into your studio or workshop. That doesn't mean you should go home and hang mirrors on your bedroom ceiling—although you can if that turns you on—what it means is that you equip your bedroom with everything you want and need to have sex. And the first thing you want and need is privacy. So your number one assignment is to have a lock installed on your bedroom door—before your child can climb out of the crib.

Some couples resist doing this because they don't want their child to feel "shut out." But locking the door teaches a child to respect privacy, as long as he or she knows that it is okay to knock on the door if they really need you. If you're having a hard time believing that a locked door is the best thing for your relationship and your child's well-being, just talk to some of the people whose kids have walked in while they were having sex. While it is true that most children aren't traumatized by this nearly as much as their parents, it's also easy to avoid.

I also find that the couples who lock their bedroom door tend to have spontaneous sex more often.

Once you've taken care of "workshop security," you should both pack your own "this is all I need to have sex" gym bag or suitcase. Some items to include in your bags are lubricant, sexy lingerie, condoms or your diaphragm (if you're not on the pill and you don't want to get pregnant again right now), sex toys, (including a backup set of batteries), and massage oil.

If your bedroom does not have a private adjoining bathroom, make sure your bags include some moist towelettes or a small plastic bottle of water and wash cloths.

Your "sex kit" should be able to serve two purposes. One, you can go into the bedroom, lock the door, and have everything you need to have sex ready and available, which increases the ease and likelihood of having sex.

Two, you can grab your sex kits and take them with you for a "nooner" at the nearby motel while your child is in day care or school, or for a planned outing.

In addition to your sex kit, I also suggest keeping a radio or stereo in your bedroom to create a sexy mood and also to serve as background noise.

Tips to Make It Better and Better

Let the great sex begin!

First of all, if at this moment, you are not highly educated or proficiently skilled in the art of lovemaking, you are in the vast majority of the population. Learning the intricacies of the human body and psyche, and having an opportunity to practice and perfect talents and techniques, present no small share of difficulties. You're not going to learn from porno material, that's for sure, and you're not going to learn, most of the time, from Mom and Dad. You're not going to learn in school.

Most people's sexual education is based predominantly on their own experiences. If you're dedicated to the process of paying attention and learning how to improve, your own experience can take you a long way. But it can't take you all the way, because there are some incredibly erotic body spots that you may never even touch upon, unless you happen upon them by chance, and certain techniques that you might never have known to try. That's why credible information about sex is so valuable!

Some Basics

To begin with, most of you probably know that an erection is caused by an increase of blood to the genital area. When the tissues are engorged with blood, they push the nerve endings closer to the surface of the skin and make the genital areas hypersensitive.

Everyone knows that a man has to be erect to have good intercourse. If he's totally limp, he's not going to be able to penetrate. If he's somewhat aroused, he'll be able to go through some of the motions, but it's only when his penis is actually hard that he can get the most use and pleasure out of it, and therefore give the most pleasure with it.

What most people don't know is that the same thing is true for women, in a slightly different way. A woman's clitoris is actually the tip of a 4½- to 5-inch-long organ that runs inside of the body. If the clitoris is not properly stimulated and engorged with blood prior to intercourse, a woman's chances of enjoying sex or achieving maximum pleasure or orgasm are slim to none.

Many men make the mistake of thinking that a few minutes of manual or oral stimulation should be enough to prepare a woman for intercourse. (Some women actually feel guilty if they're not aroused and ready that fast.) But it just doesn't work that way! Expecting a woman to be ready for intercourse after only a few minutes of stimulation is the equivalent of tickling a man's balls for a few minutes and expecting him to get hard and stay erect, without any other stimulation. The objective of performing foreplay on a man is to excite him and arouse him in such a way that he maintains his erection throughout the lovemaking session. The same is true for a woman, but since the majority of her "hard-on" happens inside her body, it's important to check for other signs of "readiness" (details below) before engaging in sexual intercourse or inserting a dildo.

Another myth that many men have about intercourse is that the longer they can do it, the better lovers they are. My idea of a man who can go for hours is a man who can keep me aroused for hours, be it with his fingers, his tongue, or his penis. The truth is that most women are happy to have intercourse start after they've had an orgasm, and last for about five minutes. That's particularly true if her partner is thrusting in and back out again, without doing much of anything else. However, if a man uses his penis to stimulate the vaginal opening and/or the G spot while he penetrates his partner, he can often bring her to another climax while he's inside of her. This is an amazing sensation for both lovers and most men agree that it powerfully intensifies their orgasm.

Another way to increase the pleasure principle in your lovemaking is to use more lubrication. There's no need to be skimpy here, or to worry about using too much, as long as it's a petroleum-free product. Most people don't know that using a lubricant does more than make sex smoother and more enjoyable; it also protects the vaginal tissues.

A lot of men base their sexual prowess on their ability to "make a woman wet." However, the degree of wetness doesn't have much to do with whether or not a woman is aroused. So, if a woman's vagina hasn't lubricated itself enough to make sex pleasurable, a man should not take this as a sign that he's not performing up to par. Instead, he should use lubrication and continue stimulating the woman until her genitals are engorged, her clitoris is erect, and she is ready for entry!

For Him

Perfecting your sexual intercourse skills will take your pleasure to a whole new level. Not only that, but it will dramatically increase your partner's enthusiasm and desire for lovemaking. While a lot of men put some thought and energy into giving better oral sex, very few men are concerned with improving their "fuck factor." (To be fair, most women don't put much energy into improving in this area either.) This seems to be a case of something seeming to be so obvious and simple that we think there's nothing to learn. Of course, that couldn't be further from the truth.

If you want to unlock all the magic of a woman's body, start with the outside and work your way in. Men tend to rush into intercourse because they see it as the main dish. Everything else is an appetizer or side dish. Women view it a little bit differently. For us, intercourse is more of a grand finale, sometimes followed by dessert. Although men often think that a woman's desire for longer and better foreplay is simply a "female preference," in actuality, it is a required prerequisite. Without sufficient arousal, a woman will not enjoy intercourse. Every woman is different. Some women enjoy oral sex, others want manual stimulation, and some women like sex toys. Find out what works and learn to do it very well!

The first step to pleasing a woman is locating her "hot spots." (If you missed the inside scoop on pleasure points of a woman's vagina in Chapter Seven, go back and check it out.)

The second step is learning how to stimulate her most sensitive areas. For instance, find out if your partner likes the flat part of your tongue to press against the tissues surrounding your clitoris, or whether she prefers the tip of your tongue and more of a flicking motion. Most women want a little bit of this and a little bit of that—just like men.

Once you've mastered steps one and two, start combining your efforts to double the pleasure. You might reach up and gently squeeze her nipples while you're stroking her vagina with your tongue, or you can massage the area around her clitoris with your fingers while you're penetrating her from behind. The idea is to get to know her body so well that's it's an open book to you. The more comfortable you are with your "subject matter," the more relaxed you can be while you're having sex.

That way, when you're in the heat of it, spontaneity will kick in, and each time you make love will be a new and different sensation and experience.

Another "inside scoop": One of a woman's most sensitive spots is the area right around her urethra. Knowing how to stimulate this hot spot properly will add a new element of enjoyment to your partner's vagina. Most women have no idea how enjoyable this can be because most men either pass over this area or touch it too roughly. I suggest gently massaging it with your tongue because it's too sensitive for your fingers.

You *can* use your fingers in pretty much any other area of the vagina, but you don't want to rub the clitoris to death. Use your fingers to circle the clitoral hood, massaging it and moving up and down the sides of the labia, the perineum, and inside the vaginal opening.

Too many guys do this thing that I refer to as a "finger bang." They think, "If it's enjoyable when my penis does it, it'll be enjoyable when my fingers do it." What they don't understand is that what causes a pleasurable sensation for women isn't the friction of the penis rubbing inside the vagina, it's the fact that the penis is wider than the vaginal canal so it puts pressure on the walls of the vagina, which creates the sensation of pleasure.

The vagina doesn't have any nerve endings beyond an inch or two inside, so if you're going to use your fingers, the best thing to do is insert the fingers maybe half way and put pressure on the vaginal opening and circle it around and stroke it. You don't want to bang your fingers in and out like you're looking for leftovers!

If you want to have intercourse, your goal is to get your partner as erect as you are. It's not enough just to show her you're willing and expect her to say, "Oh, boy" and be ready to hop on. Maybe that works in a small percent of cases the first couple of times you have sex, but after that it's going to take a little bit more. Once you become more familiar with each other and the initial excitement wears off, you're going to have to work for it. And it really is not a difficult thing. You just have to be able to recognize when the vagina is ready for intercourse.

The best way to know what your partner's vagina looks like when she's ready for intercourse is to take a close look after she's had an orgasm. The difference in how her vagina looks before and how it looks after will be very apparent. Her labia will be flushed with color and look swollen. The clitoris becomes enlarged by four to five times. When a woman's not aroused, the clitoris is hidden behind the clitoral hood and in order to see it you have to pull the hood back. But after a woman has an orgasm or when she's extremely aroused, you can actually see the clitoris without pulling the clitoral hood back. That's what you're aiming for before you have intercourse. I mean, you literally want your partner's hips bucking toward you signaling that she wants you—right here, right now! Some women won't want you to penetrate until after they've climaxed because that's when their vaginas are most receptive and feel the best with you inside. If you attempt intercourse before that, you're really not maximizing her pleasure and it's not going to make her want to do it again.

One more point to keep in mind is that after a woman has one or more babies, her vagina is somewhat more lax than it was pre-pregnancy. If it's not as much of a tight fit, she may not be getting the same amount of sensation as she used to. I suggest that while you're having intercourse, withdraw your penis with your hand about every ten strokes and sensuously rub it on the external areas of the genitals. Rub it up and down around the clitoris, around the vaginal opening, around the labia, and then reinsert it. And instead of just going straight in and out try doing a swirling thing, like you're swirling a cocktail.

The more of the sensitive areas of a woman's genitalia that you can incorporate during intercourse, the more pleasurable it's going to be for her. Think about it this way, when you're having intercourse and you're inserting your penis in and out, it feels good. If the woman reaches underneath and massages or holds your testicles or scratches or tickles your testicles with her fingernails, it rams up the pleasure another 25 percent. If she reaches down and grabs your penis in between strokes and maybe rubs the shaft while you're pushing inside, it's going to increase the pleasure another 25 percent, so it's just degrees of pleasure.

How excited do you want her to be? Do you want her to come back for more? The next time you approach her for sex, do you want her to say, "Yes" or do you want her to say, "Not tonight honey, I have a headache?" You know, the more pleasurable you can make it for her, the more she's going to want it.

Some men say, "How do I know what she likes?" I suggest that you ask her. Some women will tell you straight out, others who may have inhibitions about "talking about sex" will tell you with their bodies. A woman will let you know how much she's into you and what you're doing by literally reaching out and grabbing you or positioning her body in such a way to maximize her pleasure. So, if she's just lying there and she's yawning or if she's not making any noise or the noise sounds fake like *Sex in the City* kind of stuff, then she's not into it.

And by the way, contrary to what it looks like in porn films, deep penetration and repeated thrusting by themselves are the last things that will make a woman orgasm. Deep penetration feels good after the initial orgasm, because the vaginal walls become very swollen and engorged inside and you can hit an area deep inside the vagina called the "cul-de-sac," which is the deepest region of the vagina. But unless a woman has had an orgasm already, that's not going to feel very good and it might hurt.

For Her

Try to remember that when it comes to orgasms, men are the opposite of women. Once they've had an orgasm, they're ready for sleep. Once a woman has had an orgasm, she is ready for more. The vagina is constructed in such a way that once you have an orgasm, every orgasm after that is going to be stronger. A woman can have one orgasm after another, whereas a man can't. There's no downtime. A woman can literally have an orgasm and immediately start building up to the next one. That's a beautiful thing.

Every orgasm feels different and that's because they can originate from a variety of "hot spots," and combinations of those areas which are being stimulated simultaneously. They originate from different areas of the vagina. They can originate from the G spot, or they can originate from the cul-de-sac (see above). They can originate from the clitoris, the frenulum, or the U spot or any combination of those zones, so you have all these wonderful combinations. There are six spots that produce orgasm in a woman's body, so just imagine, you can have an orgasm that originates from zones one and six; two, three, and four; two and five; or five and six. That's why every orgasm feels different. Each climax originates from a different combination of spots and different types of stimulation. And, you know, if a man had this knowledge he'd be the king. He'd be talked about around town. Every woman would want to fuck him! And guess what? Your mate has this information, because I've already shared it with him. So get into it with him, and together you can have the kind of sex that makes your eyes sparkle and puts an extra lift in your step!

Some couples get into a struggle over how they approach sex, and, rather than meeting each other in the middle, they both get stubborn. This really is the same as cutting off your own nose to spite your face. There's nothing wrong with a little wine and roses, and there's also nothing wrong with just "wanting to get off," whether it's you who's feeling that way or your partner. I can't even tell you how many people (women and men) sabotage their role as lover by treating their mates as if they are perverse or not loving enough when they display their natural and honest desires for sexual satisfaction. If you're involved in a relationship that's mutually satisfactory and is committed and loving, there's nothing wrong with just wanting to get off, sometimes. You can't eat at McDonald's every day and you can't eat at Chez Maurice every day, either. So, if you're eating at Chez Maurice once or twice a week and you're eating at McDonald's once or twice a week—everyone is happy.

Now, there's one more thing I'm going to share with you, and a good many of you are not going to like it. The reality is that appearance matters. Your appearance matters to him and his appearance matters to you. It's not *the* most important thing, but it *is* important. I'm not suggesting that you sit around the house wearing your Sunday best, or that you get rid of your comfy fleece sweats. But I am saying that if you are committed to being lovers for life, you owe it to yourselves and each other to treat your physical condition and your appearance with respect.

It's not so much what you look like. It's the fact that you value yourself and your mate enough to take care of yourself. You don't have to look like a *Vogue* cover model, but you do want to have good hygiene and stay physically fit. That means exercising, maintaining a proper diet, and avoiding excessive drinking or smoking. It's not the actual act of maintaining your health and physical appearance that's sexy. It's the fact that you love and respect yourself and your partner enough to do it. Obviously this is a two-way street. That's why I recommend that couples spend some time working out together and also that they occasionally go shopping and pick out an outfit for each other.

There's nothing wrong with wanting to be visually stimulated. But remember that beauty is truly in the eyes of the beholder. Ultimately, it's how you feel about yourself that's going to project and that's going to determine how sexy your mate finds you.

Fifty Ways to Please Your Lover

Staying lovers for life isn't just about having sex, but as I've hopefully convinced you by now, great sex is the most important ingredient! Even so, we all know that being lovers extends far beyond the pleasure we give each other in the bedroom. It's very much about how we view each other, how we treat each other, and how much thought and effort we're willing to invest in our love affair. The following fifty suggestions are designed to create a deeper and broader sense of intimacy and understanding in your relationship. Many of them are simply fun. Others have a more profound effect. The idea is to continuously introduce fresh ideas and experiences into your lives. By doing this, you both grow as individuals and you create a wider, more stable foundation of good memories for your partnership.

Since there are fifty-two weeks in a year, I recommend that you take turns picking one of the fifty items on the list each week, until you've tried them all. Celebrate the final two weeks of the year by trying something "off the list"! In other words, think of something entirely new and different, and do it! Next year, repeat your favorites from the list of fifty, and replace the ones you weren't so crazy about with innovative ideas of your own!

1.   Pretend You Are Movie Stars

Dress to the nines, rent a stretch limo and tour your city. Some cities offer carriage rides, and that can be even better if the weather is good. If you know someone who loves to take photographs, hire them to capture your outing, or bring along a camera and ask the people you meet to snap a few photos of the two of you together.

2.   Escape!

Head for a cozy cabin in the woods, an action-packed visit to your favorite city, or check into a nearby luxury hotel and pretend it's your honeymoon all over again.

3.   Take a Massage or Reflexology Class Together

Touch is magic and massaging away each other's worries and pains is one of the most pleasurable ways to bond. With reflexology, you learn the pressure points on the feet that correspond to all of the other body parts. Giving each other pleasure and healing touch at the same time is "oh so nice"!

4.   Plan a Magical Vacation

Travel to a place you've both always dreamed of visiting. Let the enchantments and charms of your chosen destination sweep you away. If your children are still young, or you just had a baby, you may not want to venture very far. If that's the case, find out about the hidden treasures that are in your backyard or within an hour's drive.

5.   Take Up a New Sport Together

Learning together and playing together will awaken your zest for life. My husband and I take tennis and golf lessons and then we coach each other when we play together.

6.   Sing Your Partner's Praises

Make up a love song for your partner and sing it to him or her! You can write an "original" or change the words to an old favorite.

7.   Make Dinner an Event

Turn off the TV and turn on the music and romance. Light a few candles, dress up, and enjoy each other's company. If you're ordering takeout, serve it up on china.

8.   Share Each Other's Stories

Spend some time with your partner's family and ask them to tell you stories about him or her during childhood and teenage years. Everyone has funny stories, but everyone also has childhood stories that make them feel proud or help them to reconnect with some of their original dreams in life. This can be a very insightful way to learn more about each other and also to unearth passions or inspirations that may have gotten lost in the shuffle of "adulthood."

9.   Take a "Safe" Risk

This probably isn't the most responsible time to take up skydiving, but it is the perfect time to try something new together. If you've toyed with the idea of enrolling in a cha-cha class, or you've always wanted to learn how to ride a horse and have never done it, do it now! Not only will you feel more alive again because you're doing something that you've wanted to try, but by stepping out, you widen your experience horizon together and you take an active step away from the "parent rut."

10.   Tune into Each Other with Music

Spend an afternoon or evening sharing some musical harmony together. Check out what's available nearby and treat yourselves to your favorite music—or try something different just for a change of pace.

11.   Put on a Command Performance

Write a little skit to enact your love for your partner, or learn the strip tease dance! When one of my friends returned from a three-week study tour in Egypt she planned a special "Egyptian theme evening" for her husband. After serving an array of Middle Eastern delicacies (purchased already made at the corner specialty foods store), she slipped into a gold chain-link belly dancing costume she picked up in Cairo, flipped on the music, and turned on the passion! Be creative and have fun with this one!

12.   Play "Remember the Time?"

Take turns sharing good memories of your relationship. "Remember the time we stayed up all night watching the moon and talking?" "Remember the time your mother walked in when we were French-kissing?" "Remember the time you—"

Well, you get the idea. And so long as you're remembering, remember that this pastime is meant to recall only the good times!

13.   Make Each Other a Praise Poster

This can be as simple as a big piece of poster board with the words "I adore you" to an elaborate combination of words and photographs, or whatever your creative spirit leads you to make!

14.   Bake Cookies

Spend an afternoon or evening baking cookies together. In this fast-paced world, the simple act of slowing down enough to make home-made cookies can help you to mellow out and get back in sync with each other.

15.   Stroll Down Memory Lane

Surprise your partner by getting all those rolls of film sitting around the house developed and putting them into photo albums. You can also take this one a step further and put together a slide show, complete with music.

16.   Throw a Party

Honor your partner with a special party—just to say "I appreciate you." You may want to include some close friends, but some of the best parties for lovers are the private ones.

17.   Give Your Mate a Standing Ovation

This one's a throwback to "camp days." Whenever your partner does something great, stand up and clap for him or her.

18.   Start a New Tradition

Traditions, rituals, and ceremonies create strong bonds. Start a tradition or make up a ceremony that is meaningful to both of you and celebrate your love.

19.   Watch the Sun Rise Together

The dawning of a new day is magical and filled with hope. Enjoy this inspiring moment in each other's arms.

20.   Redecorate Your Bedroom

Create a new atmosphere in your bedroom that makes you both feel comfortable and sexy.

21.   Take a Hike

Breathe some fresh air, get your blood circulating, and enjoy the wonders of nature together at a nearby park or preserve. See how many different plants or trees are growing near the trail, and notice the variety of bird songs.

22.   Plant an Evergreen Tree

Plant a small evergreen tree as a statement for your enduring and ever-growing love for each other. If you don't have a yard, consider donating an evergreen to a neighborhood park.

23.   Surf the Web Together

Pick a topic or a place that you are both curious about or want to learn more about and see how much you can discover together from your home computer or one of the PCs at the local library

24.   Wax Poetic

Write a love poem and recite it to your partner. It doesn't matter whether it rhymes or not, the idea is to express some of your sentiments in a form that's different from the usual "store-bought" card.

25.   Broadcast Your Love

Dedicate a song to your partner on a radio request line.

26.   Make a Collage

Cut words and pictures out of magazines that represent what you love about each other. Add some ticket stubs from favorite performances, photos of the two of you together, and other "glueable" momentos and hang it in your bedroom.

27.   Schedule a "Me" Day

Plan a day when you will both go off in different directions to do whatever pleases you. When you reconnect at the end of the day, you'll have something new to share with each other.

28.   Laugh Until Your Face Hurts

Laughter is one of the best relationship medicines of all. It reduces stress and promotes emotional and physical healing because it creates an "endorphin-like" effect. Go to a comedy club, rent a funny movie, or take turns sharing your funniest memories with each other.

29.   Override Your Inner Critic

Do something for your partner that you know he or she will enjoy, but that you feel nervous or embarrassed to do. (Some examples might be stripping, masturbating, or walking around the house naked with high heels.)

30.   Go Parking

Drive to a scenic overlook, turn on the tunes, uncork the wine, and make out.

31.   Have an Indoor Beach Party

Put on your beach wear, crank up the heat, and dance barefoot to the tunes of the Beach Boys or island reggae music. This is a great way to liven up a cold and dreary winter day!

32.   Relive a Favorite Memory

Plan an evening that brings back warm memories of a vacation or special occasion you've shared together. Turn your living room into a miniature jungle to recreate the erotic vacation you had in the Caribbean, or turn your kitchen into the romantic Italian restaurant where you shared your first kiss.

33.   Try Something New in the Bedroom

Let your new skills and your imagination carry you away with this one!

34.   Plan a "Mate Appreciation Night"

Put up balloons and hang a banner that says, "You're the Best." Spend the evening showing and telling your mate how much you appreciate him or her. Top off the evening with an engraved trophy to memorialize the occasion.

35.   Seduce Your Lover

Pretend that you just met and your goal is to entice each other to "go all the way." What makes this game fun is that you're both supposed to resist for as long as you can. No matter who "wins," you both win!

36.   Share Your Dreams and Inspirations

Turn off the phone, or go for a drive and park in a secluded spot that offers both beautiful scenery and as much quiet as possible. Then simply spend some time sharing your dreams and visions for the future.

37.   Put It in Writing

Make a long list of all of the things you appreciate, adore, and love about each other. Include all the things you're proud of him or her for. Hire a calligrapher to write your list on a long scroll that you can ceremoniously present to your lover.

38.   Give Each Other Presents

Show your love by exchanging presents. They don't have to be extravagant. A simple daisy can brighten your mate's smile for days.

39.   Say, "I Love You" with Your Eyes

Sit across from your mate, holds hands, and look into each other's eyes while thinking "I love you."

40.   Tune into Each Other—Nonverbally

Spend a few hours, or even a whole day together, without speaking. This will accomplish a few things. First, you'll discover that there are very few thoughts that actually need to be spoken. Second, you'll pay more attention to your mate's body language and nonverbal cues. Third, you'll be more tuned into each other's moods and energy shifts.

41.   Bring Home Dinner

Something as simple as bringing home dinner can make your partner's day, especially if you both work and have children. If you live in a location where you can have a quality dinner delivered to your door, that's even better.

42.   Put on Your Dancing Shoes

By and large, most couples go dancing much more often in the early stages of their relationship than they do after they have children. That's really a shame because dancing together, whether it's hot and fast, slow and seductive, or sweetly romantic, reinforces your role as lovers. It's also a form of fun movement that is not sexual—although it can certainly be very suggestive!

43.   Surround Yourself with Beauty

Visit an art museum or walk through a conservatory or beautiful flower garden. Bring fresh flowers into your home and purchase a new painting or piece of artwork together. Our minds and our emotions experience pleasure in symmetry, proportion, and order. When we see beauty around us, we can often see more of the beauty within us and within each other as a couple.

44.   Cuddle Up

Cuddle up together for a lighthearted chat, a romantic or scary movie, or just to share a bowl of popcorn over the evening news. The idea is to give up a little comfort in exchange for being in each other's space and touching each other. As we get more comfortable in a relationship, we often spread out instead of curling up next to each other like we did when our relationship was new.

45.   Above and Beyond the Call of Duty

Do something for each other that really stretches your limits or inhibitions, either sexually or otherwise. Oftentimes in a committed, long-term relationship, we stop extending ourselves to please each other. Make it a point to impress each other again and stretch your own boundaries at the same time.

46.   Enlarge a "Kodak Moment"

Have one of your favorite photos together made into a poster. If you have an infant, it's great to hang a poster like this in the nursery, because every time you go in there as Mommy or Daddy, you are reminded that you're still individuals and you're still lovers.

47.   Be Kids Again

Go to an amusement park, zoo, or playground and act like a kid again. Or stay home together and play an adult version of "Simon Says" or naked "Twister."

48.   Make Something for Each Other

There's nothing like a homemade gift from the heart. Whether it's a special meal or dessert, an electronic card, or a cassette or CD with all your favorite songs, you will be doing it just for each other.

49.   Do Something Silly

Think of an activity that you consider "silly," and then do it. Obviously "silly" is open to wide interpretation. For some couples, going bowling would be a silly thing to do. For others, being silly might be roller-skating, skipping in public, making mud pies, or just making faces at each other until you both laugh.

50.   Celebrate Your Love Affair

Do something extravagant or out of the ordinary to celebrate being lovers for life.

You have just packed your baby off to college. You both can't believe it. It was just a minute ago that you went through a sensual pregnancy together. You learned so many new things about each other's bodies. You had never been so close to each other as you had during that magical nine months. Up until then you were afraid that you couldn't be so open to each other. You remember how as your pregnancy progressed you made love by spooning together and by leaning over on a pillow. You remember being so full of desire.

The house is quiet but you are not feeling alone. You love your child and have enjoyed all of the years of having a child in the home, but you are just as happy to be just you again. You have had a wonderful life together raising your child but it is not over—it is just beginning.

Your husband sneaks into the bedroom where you have been resting and thinking about your life. He bends over and kisses you behind your ear and massages your head with his fingertips. You can see the love in his eyes but you also see the lust. It is so nice to know how much you desire each other. He slips onto the bed and opens your blouse. He gently kisses your breasts and you kiss his neck as your hands rub him in that special spot at the top of his thighs. You tug at his belt . . . he stops you, kisses you, and gets up out of the bed. He walks to the window and pulls down the shades.

Instead of just reading this, go ahead and make some love!

Bibliography

Belsky, Jay, and John Kelly. *The Transition to Parenthood: How a First Child Changes a Marriage.* New York: Delacorte Press, Bantam Doubleday Dell Publishing Group, 1994.

Chism, Denise M. *The High-Risk Pregnancy Sourcebook.* Los Angeles, Calif.: Lowell House, 1997.

Curtis, Glade B., and Judith Schuler. *Your Pregnancy Week by Week.* Tucson, Ariz.: Fisher Books, 1997.

Douglas, Ann, and John R. Sussman. *The Unofficial Guide to Having a Baby.* New York: Macmillan General Reference, 1999.

Fontanel, Beatrice, and Claire d'Harcourt. *Babies: History, Art, and Folklore.* New York: Harry N. Abrams, 1997.

Gadpaile, Warren. *The Cycles of Sex.* New York: Charles Scribner's Sons, 1975.

Harper, Barbara. *Gentle Birth Choices: A Guide to Making Informed Decisions.* Rochester, Vt.: Healing Arts Press, 1994.

Sears, William, and Martha Sears, with Linda Hughey Holt. *The Pregnancy Book: A Month-by-Month Guide.* New York and Toronto: Little Brown and Company, 1997.

Shannon, Jacqueline. *The New Mother's Body Book.* Chicago: Contemporary Books, 1994.

Index